*"This is a story of one w[...] light, from fear to faith, fr[...] to find it. Some books se[...] such book."*
**Rev. J. R. Kearns, Founder of Hope Community Church, Aintree**

*"Having grown beyond her struggles with mental health, the author is a shining example of perseverance, determination and dedication. I wholeheartedly commend 'Freedom at Last' to you."*
**Carl Brettle, CEO of Neighbourhood Prayer Network**

*"An honest, humble and bold story of a journey through periods of pain and despair. Hope in a God who was not ashamed to identify with the parts of her life that she wanted to hide."*
**Rev. D. Connelly, Founder of Gathered to be Scattered**

# Freedom at Last
A Journey from Debilitating Thoughts and Feelings to Freedom

Copyright © 2023 Jean Dobson

The moral rights of the author have been asserted.

Apart from any fair dealing for the purposes of research or private study, or criticism or re-view, as permitted under Copyright, Design and Patents Act 1998, this publication may only be reproduced, stored or transmitted, in any form or by any means, with prior permission in writing of the publishers, or in any case of the reprographic reproduction in accordance with the terms of licences issued by the Copyright Licensing Agency. Enquiries concerning reproduction outside these terms should be sent to the publishers.

PublishU Ltd.

www.PublishU.com

Scripture from the Holy Bible, New International Version®, NIV®. Copyright © 1973, 1978, 1984, 2011 by Biblica, Inc.™ Used by permission of Zondervan. All rights reserved worldwide.

All rights of this publication are reserved.

With thanks to the following:

Carl Brettle who recognised I had a story to write.

Reverend Lee Jennings who encouraged me to write my first sentence.

Matt Bird—my amazing coach.

Ruth Mulhall, my prayer partner and iron-sharpens-iron, long-suffering editorial friend.

(Father) Freddie Jackson, an Anglican priest, mentor and friend who told me about God's amazing love.

The staff, doctors and nurses of the Westmoreland GP Centre who have been part of my journey, for their expertise and support.

And most of all, my beloved husband, who has lived with me through the trials, ups and downs of mental health to the freedom I now enjoy. An amazing husband, best friend and man of God.

# CONTENTS

**Forward**

**Introduction**

**Chapter One**       Early Beginnings

**Chapter Two**       The Teenage Years (Growing up, sunny blue skies)

**Chapter Three**       The Workplace and Disaster Strikes

**Chapter Four**       Disaster and Debilitation

**Chapter Five**       London, Light, Dreams and Visions

**Chapter Six**       Ministry, ForMission, Freedom in Sight

**Chapter Seven**       The Mental Maze, Giants Defeated

**Chapter Eight**       Self-Awareness

**Chapter Nine**       The Jigsaw Pieces (Freedom is just around the corner)

**Chapter Ten**       Freedom

**Conclusion**

**About the Author**

JEAN DOBSON

# **FOREWORD**

Aside from the fields of medicine, science and research, "pandemic" wasn't a common word we used – until recently. A pandemic is bigger than an epidemic; it's not localised but globalised. The reality is, there is a bigger pandemic in our nation, the western world, and even potentially across the globe, than Covid-19 ever was. It worries more people, traps more people, creates more fear in people, makes more people sick, and indirectly kills more people.

It's the pandemic of busyness.

It's a restlessness in our souls and bodies that drives us to do more, achieve more and receive more. It's fed by the unrealistic expectations of self and others to do more, be more and produce more.

The other feeder to this is the underlying background to our own lives – our upbringing, the triumphs, the tragedies. There's a desire to please those we love and the hiding away inwardly from those who have caused us hurt.

The result of all of this is the next pandemic – the plethora of mental health battles that many of us face on a daily basis.

There is an invitation by Jesus to come to Him, with the weightiness of our baggage, and allow Him to lighten the load:

*"Come to Me all you who are weary and carry heavy*

*burdens and I will give you rest. Take My yoke upon you. Let Me teach you, because I am humble and gentle at heart, and you will find rest for your souls"* (Matthew 11:28, 29).

It isn't an overnight process. My own experience tells me that we often like to take the weighty baggage back again, without realising it.

Jean's story is also one that invites you into her early days in the outskirts of post-war Liverpool, through the joys and sorrows of childhood and the tragedies and triumphs of adult life. However, through the constant love and example of faith in her maternal grandmother and the unexpected lifelong friendship with an older priest, it is a story of how by keeping company with Jesus, she has been able to live freely.

The Bible tells us that all of us were once in the darkness. Indeed, maybe you are there today dear reader; all of us were in a pit which we could not lift ourselves out of. However, through the love and sacrifice of Jesus Christ, He lifted us and when we accept this truth in faith, we are indeed brought into freedom from the darkness by Jesus Himself. Jean's story also tells of the darkness which can descend like fog when we least expect it and the pit of mental breakdown which can seem so impossible to climb out from. Maybe, dear reader, you are in this darkness today, or someone you dearly love is and as a result you have picked up this book from a place of desperation. Jean's story tells us that hope in these dark moments is not lost. She shares of her courage to accept the help of doctors and medication, as well as the grace of God's goodness, to lift her from that dark pit of despair to a place of hope and freedom. John's Gospel begins with the thrilling words that,

> *"The Light shines in the darkness, and the darkness, can never extinguish it"* (John 1:5).

Jean's story declares how the darkness never overcame the light within her, no matter how close it came.

I have had the privilege of simultaneously serving alongside Jean in church ministry, witnessing first-hand her administrative excellence spanning from those early career days, as she often overcompensated for my incompetence and also the honour of serving as Jean's pastor in recent years. Jean's heart is for the freedom which she has experienced, to be experienced by all those she meets and indeed is the heart behind this book.

My prayer is that as you read this endearing life story, you will know the freedom which Christ can offer in your own challenges. He offers hope in the challenges being faced by those whom you know and love. Self-help can only get so far; medicine, doctors and talking therapies definitely help – but true freedom comes in the soul, and the only way to that is through Jesus Christ. In the words of Jesus Himself:

> *"So if the Son sets you free, you are truly free"* (John 8:36).

Rev. Lee Jennings

Aintree, September 2023

JEAN DOBSON

# INTRODUCTION

There are moments in life when an opportunity comes our way to step out of the boat and do something we have never done before. Writing my story has been one such opportunity. For each of us, the Covid pandemic will have its own story to tell. Like most people, being incarcerated (for husband Phil and myself) caused life as we had known it to come to a standstill. Daily statistics of the toll the disease was taking added to the challenges we all faced. Out of that came some heart-warming stories of random acts of kindness, acts of bravery, and a sharing in our common humanity.

For me, this was the balance which tipped the scales to seriously put pen to paper and write my story. As the statistics increased of another pandemic – that of the increased challenge of mental health – my heart ached and I had the conviction I needed that I had a story to tell. "Freedom at Last" tells the story of my life-long battle with mental health. There were times of great joy in my life; at other times they were overshadowed by deeply disturbing thoughts and feelings; painful memories I was unable to make sense of. Two and two were not making four. Thankfully, I was able to work through it all, maintaining full-time employment right up to retirement, which was one of my goals. I knew I would get there. I wouldn't be defeated.

Physical pain is relatively easy to diagnose and treat. The source presents itself quite clearly. Mental pain is something quite different. It is hidden, often to the person themself. However, as physical pain is treatable, so is mental health. I applaud the skills of the consultant who treated me when I was hospitalised and especially those of the team at my local general practice. We are complex human beings, which we possibly only appreciate when something goes wrong – a broken leg, a blocked sinus, blurred sight and even when our mind doesn't function as fully as it should. I share my journey through brokenness, mental pain and into freedom. I trust it will give you some insight into mental health and hope for the journey.

## CHAPTER 1
# EARLY BEGINNINGS

The prompting to write came to me several times. It initially started whilst sitting on an airplane, due to head off to Southern Spain for a two-week retreat. Our flight had been delayed briefly by another plane blocking our runway. In what seemed like no time at all, thoughts and ideas began to fill my mind as we awaited take-off. I could see pages of a book covering my journey from debilitating thoughts and feelings into freedom – a long and challenging journey. The inspiration to write was the hope that my journey would create hope for others. Like all journeys, mine has a beginning and an end, with so much experienced along the way.

Life can begin full of hope and certainly in early childhood, days can appear sunny every day and skies always blue. My early childhood was no exception. I was born in Aintree, Liverpool, to a family of four – my Mum, my Dad, my Nan and Pop. Nan and Pop played formative roles in my early life. I was the first of two children to be born to the family. Apparently giving birth to me was a little challenging for Mum. In labour for some time before my birth, Mum was bed-bound for the two weeks following my arrival. She needed Dad to carry her to the bathroom during those weeks. Immediately on arrival I was popped into an airing cupboard in the bedroom. My dad hurried downstairs to let Nan and Pop know that they had a granddaughter. Nan rushed upstairs, concerned to know where the baby was. Pointed in the direction of the airing cupboard, Nan was my rescuer and cradled me in her arms. Oddly enough, at the moment in time when a new-born child will bond with one or both parents, I wasn't bonded with either. It was just one of those things. I was "nobody's child" and yet "everyone's" child.

With Mum's need to convalesce after giving birth, Nan was encouraged to look after me. What I learnt many years down the road was that I had been born after what had been a time of incredible sadness in the family. The second world war had broken out, Dad had been called up for active service, having proposed to Mum. They were both, by today's standards, relatively young to marry, with Mum just being eighteen years old and Dad twenty-one. Their wedding photograph tells its own story: Dad in his Air Force uniform with its slightly too long jacket sleeves and Mum looking like a very young bride. After a brief honeymoon on the Wirral, Dad sailed out to South Africa, along with the many other young recruits from this part of the world. From there, dad was flown out to India, where he served as a flight mechanic. Just prior to their wedding, Mum's brother had died tragically at the young age of nineteen. Teddy, as he was known, was in the Home Guard and was training to be a car mechanic. With good reports both from school and the workplace, he was to be set up in his own business at the age of twenty-one.

Sadly, one Friday evening, Teddy arrived home from work, feeling unwell. A visit to our family doctor and Teddy was diagnosed as having influenza. As the weekend progressed, his health deteriorated, the family doctor was sent for, and Mum's brother was admitted to our local hospital. It was at the hospital where this young man was diagnosed with spinal meningitis and died two weeks later. Years later, Mum told me that it was at this point that my nan lost the will to live. Nan's whole demeanour had changed and she permanently dressed in black. Of significance to me is that despite this tragedy having happened, my nan was the one who told me all about God and the beautiful world He had created. What my nan told me, I believed in my heart. That seed of faith kept me going through some of the later and more challenging years and has grown and grown over time. He was the wonderful Creator. Everything He created is good and the joy of being one of His children has only increased over time.

My nan kept a diary (more like a small book of her private thoughts and prayers). At the time Mum thought it appropriate I was given Nan's small book. On the day I was born, Nan wrote, "I have sung today, to our little Jean, the first time since you left us all." The family had seen a life taken, a life given, hence their choice of my name – Jean, meaning "a gift from God." Nan came back to life, so I was told, and had a reason to live again.

Pop was very much the disciplinarian of our family – a tall man with great strength of character. One look from Pop said everything I needed to know at any moment in time. The discipline came from his twenty-five years serving in the regular army in India. Pop retired from the army to marry Nan. There was for sure military order in the home, which served to be invaluable over time. My favourite time with Nan was when I would learn about family life in Melling, where Nan and her brothers and sisters grew up. Each person in the family, particularly the ladies of the household, had their own special role to play. It set a pattern for me, an understanding of family life, that we all had our part to play. That stayed with me when I later became a member of my church family.

Every now and then Pop would give me a three-penny bit. Oh joy! I would skip down the road to our local chip shop, buy three-pence worth of chips and share them with my three friends: Kenny, John and Cynthia. My other significant memory was on Sunday evenings when I would retreat to my grandparents' room for the Sunday evening service on the radio. I would love to dance when hymns were sung. My response to the music may have been a bit of a challenge for Nan (who came from a Church of England background). My response was likely a far cry from gatherings in rows of pews with orderly singing from hymn books. As I joyfully danced around their room, Nan would comment, "You'll end of up with St Vitus dance" – all said with a beautiful smile. Nan really did have the smile of an angel and the gentle quiet temperament to go with it. I loved my nan.

I have very few memories of Mum in my early years other than that Mum was the "Martha" of the family – always busy.

Dad was my tutor and best friend. The favourite photograph in my family collection is one taken of me and Dad in our backyard. In the photograph I can be seen sporting a bandaged right knee and nursing my doll. I have very little recollection of my doll other than that her eyes closed voluntarily and I remember her always being dressed in pink. Bandages were a regular feature of life for me. I was regularly being chased in fun, by either family or friends, losing my balance and falling over. I have the scars on my knees to this day – all reflections of happy times, wounds healing over and the joy of eventually becoming bandage free.

Significant times spent with Dad were learning to read and write. I was fascinated by writing down numbers, learning to count and doing sums, all aided with the use of a blackboard and easel. Added to the joy of learning to count and doing sums was reading and writing. These were such fond memories. My favourite books were stories of "Fluff" the cat and "Nip" the dog. When reciting the alphabet led to stringing words together and then reading whole sentences, a new world opened up for me, eventually leading to writing whole sentences. The love of books and reading have stayed with me throughout my life.

My main play toy was a doll's house. What joy, what excitement as I investigated each of the rooms, re-arranged furniture and imagined what kind of family would live there and what life would be like. My world of imagination took me to grand castles and stately homes. Linked to grand castles were two Scots kilts I had, one of Black Watch and the other of Royal Stewart tartans. My playmates were all born in the same year as me. Next door to us was Kenny, opposite us was Cynthia and next door to Cynthia was John. We all had great fun together on rainy days. John's mum would make a tent for us. A clothes maiden was turned upside down, a sheet thrown over the top, and we would hop inside and go on one of our adventures.

The road where we lived was, I would imagine, typical of its day. I recall it being long and somewhere we could safely play out. There were no cars around at that time.

For sure, front doors were always open. It could have been said that doors were left open as there was nothing to steal. The reality was it was post-war England and neighbours were enjoying the freedom to mingle again. It was an open and friendly community. An expression of this was a street party held in celebration of the coronation of Queen Elizabeth II. Either end of the road were two churches: one was known as Crocker's Mission, which my nan attended, and the other, bigger church building was the local Methodist church which was known for visits by the now late William Sangster. It was the Methodist church which organised the street party. It was a huge success, lots of fun and I had a role to play as part of the street queen's retinue. I wore a long dress made of turquoise taffeta and a headband made up of anemones. Seriously grown up!

All went swimmingly until just over four years after I was born. Our family grew to five members on the arrival of my brother Colin. I don't really recall anything about his birth or even the fact that Mum had been pregnant. Life had been full. When asked whether I liked my new baby brother, I wasn't honestly sure. Colin had arrived safely into the family and my life had gone on much as before. I had my own friends and had found my own place in the family. Nan had been encouraged to take me out in the pram when I was younger. As a result, Mum took on all the family household duties. For me, this meant trips to my nan's sisters: auntie Beat, auntie Flo, auntie Gert and auntie Edie. The wider family lived in fair proximity to us which meant that for me my immediate family had extended to Nan's family. A favourite photo from that time in my life was one of me sitting on a teddy bear which was on four wheels and had a handle for someone to push me along. The gift was from auntie Gert, who I spent more time with during my teenage years.

All was well. What difference to family life did my brother's arrival make? The significant difference was around logistics in the home. Immediately behind the front door was a long hallway which led to the staircase to the bathroom and bedrooms. To the left of the hall were two rooms: the front room being home to Mum, Dad, my baby brother and me. The back room was home to Nan and Pop. To the far right of Nan and Pop's room was a door to the kitchen. Here lay a problem. Access to the kitchen was via Nan and Pop's room. From my brother's arrival, Nan and Pop would take an afternoon nap. For Mum to access the kitchen to prepare bottles for my brother, etc. could mean disturbing my grandparents' afternoon nap. The family decided we needed to move to a property where the kitchen was separately accessible; better suiting family needs all round.

By this time, I was approaching my seventh birthday – a time when I would need to move to a junior school. As best I understand, that and our changed family needs, determined the time of our house move. How it all happened, I have no idea, other than one day a huge removal van turned up at our home. With great speed and efficiency, the contents of our home were packed inside the van. There was no time for goodbyes to my friends – out into the unknown, another adventure had begun. In what seemed like just a short journey, the removal van came to a halt outside twenty-eight Devonfield Road, which became our home for the next ten years. On reflection, those ten years seemed much longer – almost as though we had lived there forever. They certainly contained some happy memories. Mum may well have felt the same when leaving Aintree, where all her formative years were lived out.

A big step forward for me was starting Junior School: "big school," "real school," "proper" learning, school reports, school uniform. What was it all going to be like? Up until this point in time, life had been pretty much all fun. An early challenge I faced at Junior School was the class bully. That really was a painful experience. Like others in my class, I would arrive early for school, which meant we had time out in the playground before classes began. One morning, arriving early as usual, I heard the voice of the class bully shout out: "Don't let her join in." I was the "her" being referred to. The group responded to the bully's voice and ignored me. I was shocked to the core. This continued. My heart began to sink like a lead balloon. The joy I had had of going to school and learning just leapt out of the window. I kept it all to myself and began to live in a world of silent fear and shame, "There was something wrong with me – I wasn't accepted." This is a theme I will return to later in the book.

At the time of our move to Devonfield Road I was given a bed in my grandparents' bedroom. My brother had his own bedroom and my parents had the master bedroom. During this time of bullying, I developed a nervous cough at night which was picked up by my grandparents. The family doctor couldn't find anything physically wrong with me, and sent me for an X-ray, which also confirmed that there was nothing physically wrong with me. It was time to spill the beans. I told my dad what was happening – I was being bullied at school. As ever, Dad found words of encouragement. "Don't worry kid, this won't last forever," he said. "They'll soon find someone else to pick on." With those assuring words, Dad walked me to school each morning. We stopped at a sweet shop close to the school and Dad bought me two ounces of sweets, which I offered to the girls in the playground. The playground bullying stopped.

The rest of my years at Junior School were relatively happy. I became friends with a fellow pupil named Ann (when I one time shared with Ann's mum that I couldn't remember whether Ann's name was spelt with or without an 'e' on the end, Mrs Thomas advised that they couldn't afford the 'e' on the end. I never had a problem spelling the name from that day on!). Ann and I had some great adventures together, the greatest of which, for me, was Ann inviting me to her local church, where at fifteen I responded to the call to follow Jesus.

Post the bullying episode, I settled into life at Junior School, made some good friends and overall enjoyed the learning experience. Some of the teachers seemed like giants by comparison with the teachers in Infant School and for the most part they were very encouraging. As part of the school experience, a school holiday was arranged for those in my class. We were given the opportunity to be taken to the Lake District for a week's holiday, the week being overseen by two members of staff, who happened to be two of my favourite teachers. Quite how my parents found the money to pay for the holiday, I will never know, suffice to say I was truly thankful for the experience. We set off by coach for the Smallwood Private Hotel in Ambleside. At the time of writing, I am not sure whether the hotel still exists. I do know on a short break to the Lake District just a few years ago, the hotel still existed, although it looked pretty much abandoned. It's hardly surprising after all these years!

Ann and I shared a bedroom. We both had similar tastes in food and after breakfast would keenly examine the contents of our packed lunch for the day. Finding any sandwich which we thought we wouldn't like; we would head off to a nearby field to feed the horses. Other adventures included midnight feasts. On a different adventure we really pushed the boat out. There was an afternoon break on our day out and we both opted to invest in a Knickerbocker Glory. What a challenge that was – we failed miserably and had to leave for the coach before we were able to do justice to our purchase.

Completing the Junior School experience, two creative opportunities emerged. The first one was a part in the school nativity play. That was a bit of a damp squib for me. Having high hopes of playing the angel Gabriel, I was offered the part of an "ordinary" angel. Oh well – at least I had a part to play.

The second creative opportunity significantly outweighed the first – a part in the end of the school play. To this day, I can't remember the title of the play, other than that it was about a ladies' committee set up to eliminate the world of men (How ambitious for 10-year-olds!). We absolutely loved having the opportunity to dress up in our mothers' clothes – including hats and high heel shoes. The scene was set, the plan in place and D-day had arrived. Each member of the committee set off to their respective area to ensure that the plan had succeeded, that there were no men left, and to report back to the committee. The last lady returned only to report that the plan had failed, there was just one man left. One by one, we made our excuses to leave the gathering in search of the one man who was left. Eventually the stage was emptied – the play ended – rapturous applause was heard from delighted family and friends. My school reports were good. I had completed my 11+ examination and finished school, waiting on the outcome of the examination and whether I had done well enough to gain a place at the senior school of my choice.

JEAN DOBSON

## CHAPTER 2
# THE TEENAGE YEARS
### Growing up, sunny blue skies

To my delight, and utter amazement, when the results of my 11+ exam arrived, I discovered that not only had I passed the exam, but that I had done well enough to win a place at the school of my choice – a school I thought might well have been out of my reach. To give it its full title, Blackburne House Liverpool Institute High School for Girls (the first school for girls in Liverpool), was where I would be spending at least the next five years of my life. The building, originally the countryside home of John Blackburne, mayor of Liverpool in the eighteenth century, continues on as a place of learning for women today.

It was on to a new challenge: a new school. This time, rather than being in walking distance from home, my journey to school meant a five-mile bus journey (in fact, it meant two bus journeys). There was no direct route to school. On arrival, it was clear that the building itself had had a previous life. There was no resemblance to any school building I had known so far. It really was very different. I felt sure it could have had lots of tales to tell. My imagination had free rein. A grand staircase opened up to school rooms on the first floor, where the staff room was also located. The assembly hall also dualled as a gymnasium and our main cloakroom, referred to as "the shelter cloakroom," harked back to a bygone era.

Thankfully, my friend Ann had also won a place at Blackburne House and we made the decision to travel together. It just so happened that a neighbour's daughter was also a pupil at Blackburne House. Anne (spelled with an "e") was in her second year and her parents offered us the possibility of travelling with her for our first week. We had bus routes to work out, rules and regulations to learn and the basics of life at our new school. What a kind and helpful gesture that was. When the first day at our new school arrived, Ann and I arrived at our neighbour's home. The family had just finished breakfast and Anne's father offered to pray for us as we left for school. Initially, I felt a little embarrassed. This wasn't how the day started in my home yet it was clearly a way of life to our neighbours down the road. I felt strangely reassured as we ventured out after prayer.

The first week passed and we soon got into the drill of our new way of life. There were bigger numbers of students with three streams of us in our intake. Ann was in the top stream, I was placed in the second stream, which really was just right for me. Top streamers studied Latin. French and German were the only two languages I studied outside of English.

School assembly was quite something different. We met each morning in the main hall, after inspection. It was quite the challenge to get into the assembly hall. It took just a few short steps down from the cloakroom/washroom area into the hall. Standing to the right of those steps, each morning, was our deputy headmistress, who inspected us one by one to ensure that we were appropriately dressed for morning assembly. One morning I was asked: "Child, have you been doing something with your hair?" This was code for "Have you put a rinse on your hair/had it dyed?" Thankfully, I hadn't. I had blonde hair which had some natural highlights. Under the lights in that part of the building it may have seemed as though I had "given nature a hand!"

I did, however, make a classic mistake one morning. Looking in the mirror in the cloakroom, I decided to give my hair a bit of a lift. Influenced by the likes of Dusty Springfield, I gave my hair a bit of a back-comb and headed for assembly. My "creative bouffant" immediately caught the eye of our deputy head and I was ordered back to the cloakroom to comb it all out. Note to self – not a good idea to do that again!

Our deputy head was a good teacher and taught two of my favourite topics – R.I. and History and always brought both topics to life. Behind her desk was a copy of one of Van Gogh's paintings. It proved a pleasant distraction for me when my mind just needed a rest from processing lots of information. English Language and English Literature were my next two favourite subjects and at the bottom of the list was chemistry. I definitely had no scientific inclinations. One of my most memorable moments was during an English Literature lesson. As a class, we were enthusiastically acting out a scene from a play, storming onto the teacher's platform. Shortly afterwards our headmistress appeared in the classroom doorway and summoned our teacher. We later discovered that our energetic actions had caused the ceiling in our headmistress's room to shake (her office was directly below our classroom).

Another odd moment happened during the winter at school. We were required to play out in the school playground at lunchtimes. For whatever reason, a group of us decided to stay indoors and found our way into the shelter cloakroom (which at lunchtimes was out of bounds). We decided to try on each other's coats for a bit of fun. We were different shapes and sizes. The bell went for lessons. We abandoned our coats as we headed back for afternoon lessons. As the end of the school day came, I headed back to the cloakroom only to find to my horror that my coat was nowhere to be seen. After a thorough search I headed to the secretary's office to report my loss. Given that I had been in the cloakroom at out-of-bound hours, I was advised to look sorry for myself before our deputy head was brought in.

Together we searched every nook and cranny of the building. For sure my coat had gone. It was winter and all that was left in the cloakroom was a selection of lab coats and plastic macs. "Well, child," exclaimed our deputy head, "we have to get you home. You will need to wear a lab coat and put on a plastic mac to keep you dry." Suitably attired for my somewhat embarrassing journey home, I was reminded that I needed to put on my school beret. I managed, in a moment's panic, to put it on inside out, with my name label sewn right across the middle. Our deputy head managed to keep a straight face as I put my beret back on, right side out, and headed for the bus home. My coat was never recovered. A costly mistake on my part and even more costly for Mum and Dad who had to invest in a new winter coat for me that met school regulations. I learnt a few unexpected life lessons from the experience.

Senior school opened many different learning experiences for me. I discovered that I was reasonably good at sport and was chosen to play for my school in the rounders, netball and hockey teams. At the end of each year, team members were awarded a school badge, which was usually worn on our school shorts. I loved these sports and developed friendships with members of the different teams. An additional bonus was the award of school colours. Our school colours contained the school motto, written in Latin, which read "Non nobis solum sed toto mundo nati," which translates to "Not for ourselves alone, but for others are we born." This opened my mind up to the wonderful world my nan had taught me about and that I had a role to play in helping others. To be honest, a bit further down the road I began to take this to the extreme, where I almost ruled myself out, focussing on the needs of others. I will elaborate on this further on in the book. How easily we can unintentionally take something out of perspective, to our own detriment.

Outside of school life, I attended church each week and at fifteen sensed the call to follow Jesus. I attended my local Anglican Church, St John the Evangelist, Rice Lane. Being the age I was at the time, I tended to sit near the back of the church, along with members of my peer group. Whilst it did give us a bit of freedom in that we weren't under the eagle eye of the vicar, we could also pass the occasional sweet round when hunger pangs set in. Being at the back of the church had special significance for me. I loved the long and solemn walk down to the altar rail in front of the main altar. Overcoming self-consciousness, I would take in what was the sacred moment of receiving the bread and the wine or a blessing – as was the case until confirmation. The mystery and the majesty of my faith was becoming real.

I took confirmation classes, then the day of my confirmation came – the evening of Tuesday, 27 March

1962. I felt a great sense of excitement and was thrilled at being clothed in white. I chose a white, broderie anglaise, boat-neck dress, which had a modestly full skirt. To accompany the dress, I wore a pair of medium height, white chisel-toed leather shoes, with a leather pompom decorating the front of the shoe. The occasion and the significance of the moment is as clear in my mind today as it was then – "Accepted in the Beloved."

Confirmed by the then Bishop of Liverpool, we were all given a small red handbook "In His Presence." Inside the front cover were the words:

> *"Anyone who wants to serve Me must follow Me, because My servants must be where I am. And the Father will honour anyone who serves Me"* (John 12:26).

There was a final verse at the end of that page

> *"...But if you remain faithful even when facing death, I will give you the crown of life"* (Revelation 2:10).

I have that little red book to this day. In the back pages are promises I made to God and my favourite scriptures at the time. (I have yet to find the time to explore those scriptures to see how my perspective/understanding has changed over the years). My first communion was on Mothering Sunday which, for some very odd reason, happened to fall on what was known as April Fool's Day, Sunday, 1 April. This for sure fooled one person – the one who had come to kill, steal and destroy!

An additional blessing at this time was church youth club. St John's Youth Club was held on a Monday evening, and I discovered a second youth club, which was held on a

Friday evening at another church further down the road. A blessing in more ways than one, I was able to attend both. The Friday night youth club was run by two brothers. As I recall, both brothers were teachers: one definitely taught English. No surprise, drama featured in Friday night's youth club activities. I discovered I had another area of interest and made even more new friends. Clearly, something fresh was being awakened within me from the days I used to sing hymns and dance in my grandparents' room when we lived in Aintree. Amongst other activities, the youth club put on an Old Time Musical. For the production the girls created their own hats out of straw sunhats which they decorated with handmade colourful crepe paper flowers. I had a solo part singing "My Old Man" and a duet with one of the boys to "Daisy, Daisy." Somehow our production came to the attention of our main Liverpool evening newspaper. A reporter came along, the cast had our photographs taken and a small article appeared alongside the photograph. We had become famous!

My invitation to the Friday night youth club came via an unexpected route. The former class bully from junior school, the one who had on more than one occasion challenged school friends not to play with me, invited me. This was quite remarkable and quite unexpected. What happened as a consequence of this, is testimony to how wonderful God is and how He can turn bad situations around for good. We were both invited to play lead parts in a one-act play: "The Happy Journey to Trenton and Camden" by Thornton Wilder. There was no scenery. There was just half a dozen chairs. It was a role reversal for both of us. The former bully played the part of my married daughter who had just lost a baby in childbirth. I played her mother.

Mother (me) and father, along with two other siblings, made the journey from Camden to Trenton to support their daughter. Seated on four chairs, two in front, and two behind, the family shared the joys and sorrows of life as they motored along to New Jersey. When the destination was reached, mother and daughter embraced each other. The play was entered into a youth clubs' drama competition. We came second in the competition. Our acting skills were praised and we were encouraged that, had we not taken on so ambitious a project, we may well have come first. What was so remarkable was the fact that on the day of the actual performance, both my opposite number and I were so overcome with emotion at the reunion, we ended up in floods of tears as we embraced each other. Our paths never crossed again.

With the march of time, my secondary school education was to come to an end. What was next? Was I to stay on in further education? Would I be clever enough to study further and would my parents be able to foot the bill? All these questions ran through my mind as my final year came round. The answer came in an unexpected way at the close of morning assembly. As we came out of assembly, I was drawn to the main noticeboard and to an advert for Millbank College of Commerce. The college was to open that September, offering a one-year secretarial training course. The seed was sown – new horizons could open. To my mind, a year was neither here nor there, and if successful, I would have additional skills to offer in the workplace. I applied, was offered a place and never looked back. By God's grace and thanks to the fantastic college staff, skills were honed that have lasted throughout my working life and beyond.

A new chapter in my life opened as I began my year's secretarial training at Millbank College. I loved it. What an adventure. A brand-new college had opened with a brand- new experience. I wasn't quite sure how I would manage writing in shorthand. Joy came onto me one day on the bus to college when I discovered that I was able to translate words on advertisements on hoardings into shorthand outlines. Typing was a different challenge. Manual typewriters were the order of the day. Speed tests were fascinating. The clatter of keys I found hilarious as we were given orders to start typing. I really had to focus on the task at hand, rather than the clicking sound of the keyboards to ensure that I finished my task and reached the target speed.

Further adventures opened-up as we formed a college netball team with two players from Malawi. They were fantastic. I can still see their smiles and feel their energy to this day. We also managed to put on a Christmas party for "under-privileged" children. Another clear memory was that of having the courage to put my idea to my class teacher, then presenting the idea to the college principal. His response ran something like, "Well my dear, if you can find any under-privileged children in Liverpool, you are welcome to put on a Christmas party." We did. Basic administrative skills kicked in as lists appeared on classroom noticeboards throughout the college, asking students to tick which food items they were able to bring: jellies, cakes, sandwiches, crisps, lemonade. The response was amazing. I can't fully remember how the event went, other than that it went well. There were lots of smiley faces. It was both a joy and a relief to see the happy faces – a reward in itself. The unexpected icing on the cake was a letter received by the college principal, expressing thanks on behalf of the children for the afternoon they had spent with us.

The college year began to draw to its close, exams loomed up, and we were addressed by several prospective employers. I recall most of them were representatives from local banks/insurance companies. How blessed we were in the 1960s – a time of full employment. It felt a bit like the world was our oyster and that we had the choice of who we would like our employer to be. Again, I was thankful for God's grace. I finished the year well and was drawn to the Royal Insurance Company with whom I was offered a place within the organisation and began training in the typing pool. Thankful for the career advice we had received, it was clear to me that to progress from college to holding a secretarial position, I would need to get some basic office experience under my belt.

The Royal Insurance proved a great training ground. From the typing pool, I was offered a post within the company's Continental Department. My role was to work with the departmental translator. He was a lovely gentleman, who reminded me a bit of Mr Pastry. I marvelled at his skill at translating from one language to another. The senior secretary, who worked to the Head of Department, also operated our telex machine. On the odd occasion I stood in for her and was asked to take dictation from the head of department. I kid you not – I was terrified. He was a tall man with a powerful presence. I could feel my knees knock, my heart pounding, hoping that I would be able to transcribe my shorthand notes. Thankfully, all went well, and as my confidence grew and I gained experience, I had a sense that before too long it would be time for me to spread my wings and to look for a "proper" secretarial post.

JEAN DOBSON

## CHAPTER 3
# THE WORKPLACE AND DISASTER STRIKES

As I write, I realise afresh how good God has been to me. With a sense of restlessness, I sensed it may be time to move on. With the Spirit's prompting, I scanned through the Situations Vacant column of the Liverpool Echo. Surprise, surprise, my eyes fell on a situation that had become vacant at a company local to home. I am by nature an optimistic person. Appreciating that my work experience was limited, I had enough confidence to put together an application for the job advertised, which was as secretary to the Commercial Manager of the company. The interview went well, and to my delight I was offered the job. Another adventure was about to begin.

The building in which I worked had previously been a house and was at the front of the company's premises. Behind the house were the production areas, where tins, cans, metal boxes and drums were made. With my job came my own office. It was a long, narrow room, with just one window at the far end. I realised, as I sat at my desk on that first day, that I for sure had set myself a challenge. With the safe environment of a department behind me, it was make or break time. The first few months were a challenge, however with time I got into the routine of secretarial life. My boss was a very pleasant man, clearly loved his work and was a joy to work with. I learned new skills of managing the boss's diary, keeping files up-to-date and making sure he had all the papers he needed for his various appointments. Taking dictation, and transcribing outlines into letters was an equal joy. All that I had learned at college was now fitting into place and the added bonus was that I was paid a salary at the end of the month. How good was that?

The staff Christmas dinner dance proved an additional bonus from this company. I'd never been to one of those before. I was a little apprehensive – what to wear and the usual sort of questions through my mind. What turned out to be an unexpected blessing for me was that as a hobby I had taken up ballroom dancing. I had won medals in both modern ballroom and Latin American dancing (Latin American dancing at that time was a far cry from what it is today!). You can probably guess what is coming: After dinner, came the invitation to dance. We were graced by the presence of our chairman at this particular event and I had the privilege of being invited to take to the dance floor with him for a waltz. I was very relieved that I had some experience under my belt. The chairman was a tall, slim and graceful dancer. Being whisked around the dance floor, I felt like I was in a dream. It was a wonderful moment I won't easily forget.

Time marched on and a few years down the road I sensed it was time to move on again. Turning, as ever, to the Situations Vacant in the Liverpool Echo, I was drawn to an advertisement for a secretarial position with a large, international company which had a factory on the Kirkby industrial estate. I now had something of a curriculum vitae together and sent off for an application form. From the advertisement, it was clear that the job would entail a big jump in responsibility for me and yet it seemed just the right next move (were my application to be successful).

With the somewhat lengthy application form completed and posted, I waited anxiously to find out whether I would even be interviewed for the post. To my delight, I was invited to attend for interview. The big wide world of the workplace seemed even bigger as I turned up for my interview. I can't remember the content of the interview, other than that I was nervous and turned up in what I hoped would be suitable dress for the occasion – a brown and black herringbone suit, accompanied by a yellow, short sleeved crocheted top. I certainly felt the part as I took dictation from the man who subsequently became my boss and life-long friend. It was a bit of a cliff-hanger as at the end of dictation, I learnt that there were a number of other applicants being interviewed for the post. Post formal interview, I was shown to the office of the head of personnel and sat in her secretary's office to transcribe my shorthand notes. The whole process over, I headed home and waited for the outcome.

What a blessing as the long-awaited letter arrived and I learnt I had been offered the job. The icing on the cake was that my salary doubled in just one move. I found this quite amazing, given that at the time I had so brief a C.V. How good is God! Further down the road my boss explained the reason for my appointment. He had approached the interview from two perspectives, either to recruit someone, like his secretary who was moving down South and was an older lady and would bring considerable experience to the post, or take a risk and employ a younger person, who although lacking experience, could grow into the role. That younger person turned out to be me. We often joked down the road of how it was his training that saw me develop and grow in the workplace as I did. On reflection, we both learned from each other as down the line, he helped me through some very difficult years. So too I had the privilege of doing the same for him.

At this point in time, life couldn't have been better. Door after door had opened for me in the workplace and I had a growing number of friends. My new role certainly had its challenges. The scope of the job was such that for my first week in post, my boss took a week's leave so that I could familiarise myself with the company, his role, his management team and draw on the experience of his secretary who had been with him for many years. The company also had its own inter-connecting telephone lines between the various locations in the United Kingdom.

I had a week to take it all in whereafter it became time to take up my role. The outgoing secretary was very kind and helped me through the intricacies of the role. It was for sure a challenge and I had a lot to learn. On one occasion, we had a visitor from one of the company's factories in France. Having an "O" level in French, my boss dictated a letter which I was invited to translate into French. Thankfully all went well, and our guest was able to read what together my boss and I had written.

A similar challenge came when we had a visit from the company's parent plant in New York. Knowing the American love of English history, my boss set me a fresh challenge. The challenge was to research the history of the area where the company had established its factory and write up a paper for our American guest to read. It was a fascinating journey for me. I have always loved history and thoroughly enjoyed the experience.

In the mix of everything else, I was also given the opportunity to visit the company's other locations in the United Kingdom – a week's learning curve. It was fascinating as well as educational. I met some amazing and interesting people during the week and some entertaining company over breakfast at the hotel where I was based.

Fully briefed, my working life took off. I hardly slept a wink for the first twelve months in post. There was so much to learn. With time I grew into the role and enjoyed every minute, including one occasion when the company chauffeur was patiently waiting to take my boss to the train station. I found myself on my hands and knees searching for a document in the archive under my boss's bookcase. Thankfully I was able to retrieve the document and my boss arrived, as best I understand, by the skin of his teeth to catch the train to London.

I write in detail about my time with this company as it was a significant time in my life and the company ethos so matched my heart and understanding of family. My nan sowed the seeds in childhood, I saw the importance of family and how we all have our part to play. The significance of this particular company to me was its paternalistic expression as an employer. Staff were looked after well and were well rewarded.

An aspect of the company's life was the social life which it offered. My boss, in addition to being the Deputy Plant Manager and Plant Engineer, also held the position of Chairman of the Recreation Society. Surprise, surprise! Not before too long, I was invited to become secretary to the Recreation Society and became involved in every aspect of the society's life. It was lots of fun, and also work that I could do in "work time." The society's activities included organising what was known as the annual "Bonus Dance," the Children's Christmas Party and the Social Club. The "Bonus Dance" was held each year as the company's bonus was declared. Depending on the company's profits during the course of a year a bonus would be declared, which would translate into a one-off payment for every employee. To celebrate, the company also paid to hire a venue, where there would be a disco and general rejoicing at the company's success. It was open to all employees and was known as "The Bonus Dance."

The company also had a badminton club and a cricket team. I became life-long friends with one of the badminton players, who worked across the site in the Research Laboratory. Our friendship also saw us become involved in what became the company's cricket league. The men didn't trust one another to score, so we learnt the noble art of scoring. It was great fun and we were rewarded by putting together a women's team to play the men at the end of the season.

A big challenge came with the inter-factory sports day. I'm not too sure how this came about, although I have a feeling my boss may well have had something to do with it. This particular year, the Kirkby plant was to be the host. The men had their football team and my friend and I were invited to put together a netball team, which we managed to do. We arranged to be trained at a local school by one of the P.E. teachers who very kindly gave us of her time. As the sports day neared, Roberta and I set about making our netball tunics. We agreed on a pattern and set to work. The piece de resistance was sowing yellow daisies onto the tunics. We were pretty pleased with our efforts and thought we'd done a reasonable job (more so than our efforts on the netball pitch). We had done well to put a team together and although we lacked the experience of some of the other teams who played competitive netball, at least we managed to compete and made a reasonable first of the day.

Roberta and I had a similar sense of humour and loved to take people under our wing. One such person was our training officer who was a firm favourite of ours and was a member of the badminton club. From the south, he commuted each week up to the Kirkby plant. Not quite knowing how to take Scouse humour, he didn't believe there was such a thing as a "Scouse" pie ("Scouse" is a stew typically made from chunks of meat, usually beef or lamb, with potatoes, carrots and onion. It can be topped with a layer of puff pastry). We treated him to lunch one day, taking him to a pub not too far away from the factory and one we knew served up "Scouse" pies at lunchtimes. Another fun moment, for us, was making our training officer an "apple pie" bed (a practical joke where a bed is folded in a way so that a person's legs cannot be stretched out). Roberta had arranged a "pre-hospital" party for me at the hotel where our training officer resided during the week. One of our management team found a piano in the room we had been allocated for the evening. We had such fun that night as he entertained us with his skills on the piano. The fun extended (for Roberta and myself) over to the next day when Gerry turned up in my office to ask who had sneaked up to his bedroom and made the apple-pie bed. Who could it have been?

At a time when life couldn't have been better – a great job, great friends and a very full life, disaster struck. Who would have thought? It really was inconceivable that anything could go wrong. It took both me and everyone else by surprise.

All seemed well as I set off for a summer holiday in Spain with a friend, her mum and her mum's friend. Just weeks before our holiday I began to develop a sore throat, which turned into tonsillitis. This had become a weakness over the years. On reflection, an obvious sign I had exhausted energy levels would be the annual sore throat which would turn into tonsillitis. This particular year, as we headed off to Spain and our holiday unfurled, the pain of my infected tonsils increased. Thankfully, I had a friend whose mum's friend was a nurse. She had packed away a variety of medications, one of which relieved the pain of my infected tonsils. This was, for me, a wake-up call. On a number of occasions, our family doctor had recommended I part company with my tonsils. I regularly resisted. This experience on holiday caused me to change my mind. Holidays, at that point in time were important to me. I worked hard all year, as did my friends. We were all ready for our summer holidays and time to recharge our batteries. Thought to self – maybe it is time for me and my tonsils to part company?

On return from holiday, I arranged an appointment with my GP who subsequently arranged an appointment for me with a local ENT consultant. Can you imagine the impact when I turned up for my hospital appointment, having resisted surgery for years? The consultant took one look down my throat and explained: "I've never seen a pair like that before, they will need to be removed."

Arrangements were put in place for me to be admitted for surgery. Was this a challenge for someone who was just twenty-one years of age? Apparently so! I had a conversation with the factory nurse who advised that from twenty-one years upwards, the danger was that a patient could bleed to death. Cause for celebration with my Kodak friends. Roberta organised two weeks of nights out, ahead of surgery, which included a trip for a group of us to a swimming pool, followed by a Chinese meal. The memory of that Chinese meal will live with me forever! Brought up in a home with a traditional English diet, Chinese food was way out of my experience. Roberta managed to trick me, and we ended up in a restaurant in an area of Liverpool known as "China Town." No compromise. It was Chinese food or nothing. I was hungry and tucked into my first-ever "Chinese" meal – Chicken fried rice – and thoroughly enjoyed every mouthful!

The operation went ahead successfully and in next to no time everything went pear-shaped. It seemed that within days after surgery and discharge from hospital, my clothes began to feel tight. They were certainly too tight for comfort. I had never dieted in my life – never even thought about it. Suddenly I had an unexpected challenge. I needed to think about my diet and how to lose the weight I seemed overnight to have acquired.

At that time, there was a weight loss programme advertised in a women's magazine. I picked up a copy of the magazine and pored over the content. There was even a calculator included with the magazine, together with a handbag-sized booklet. As I did with everything in life, I dived into the weight loss programme whole-heartedly. I can't perfectly remember whether the diet was low carbohydrate or low calorie or something else. I remember Brazil nuts having a particularly good numerical value, were nutritious and filling and fitted into a low carbohydrate group. Each food from A-Z had a unit value. To lose weight, the goal was to achieve a target of a certain number of units each day. As I write this, I realise how goal oriented I can be. If I set myself a goal, it will be met. And so, the goal was set. Initially, I set myself the minimum goal, then increased it as time progressed.

With time, I began to lose weight rapidly and dropped down at least one dress size. For sure, clothes fitted comfortably. The subsequent challenge was that I didn't know how to let go. I had been so shocked by the sudden weight gain, I kept going with the diet plan. I distinctly remember one afternoon in the office being so light-headed from eating so little for lunch that I thought I was going to faint. The subsequent consequence of this continued weight loss was that I developed amenorrhea. It was shock and horror – what was I to do? From a visit to my GP, I was advised that the medical condition was not uncommon in someone who had had significant weight loss and that the condition would right itself. I was faced with a dilemma and doubt crept into my mind. What if our family doctor was wrong?

At this same point in time, a friend of mum's, who was a nursing sister, based at one of our local hospitals, shared that her consultant was developing hormone therapy. This might possibly help. Would I be interested? I take full responsibility for the consequences of not listening to the advice of our family doctor; I enrolled for hormone replacement therapy. It was the worst thing that could have happened in my life, or so it felt in retrospect. The impact of the treatment was that it brought on the symptoms of the menopause. I became out of control emotionally. I would cry at the least thing, colour unexpectedly, would consume vast quantities of chocolate at certain times of the month and what was, for me, one of my worst moments, I shouted at my brother for pinching an apple out of my lunch box. My response to his actions scared me. I shouted at Colin: "If you do that again, I'll kill you." I was mortified by those words and determined I needed help. My next port of call was back to my GP who diagnosed that I was suffering from depression and needed medication. I take full responsibility. The next thing that happened was in fact a chemical explosion – the consequences of mixed medication which saw me in hospital – for quite some time.

JEAN DOBSON

## CHAPTER 4
# DISASTER AND DEBILITATION

How did that "chemical explosion" take shape? What was it like? What thoughts went through my mind, and how did I come to be in hospital? As described towards the end of the previous chapter, the consequence of undergoing hormone therapy was that I experienced frightening thoughts and emotions. To be honest, everything just went out of control. Prior to hormonal treatment, I would say I had been a reasonably balanced individual, gregarious, outgoing and loving life. The strong negative emotions which I began to experience were very much out of character. I would fight hard to keep emotions under control. It really was a battle. I would suddenly feel a previously unexperienced emotion bubbling up under the surface. I had no idea what it was, other than the outcome would be what might be described medically as a "hot flush." In identifying the most predominant emotion now, I would say it was primarily anger. I didn't want to be angry. Anger was a horrible thing. To this day, I struggle when I see people burst out in anger over something. As the battle raged, I would suddenly cry uncontrollably. What had happened to the happy individual I had been, not all that long ago?

Whilst all this was going on, I was thankfully managing to function in the workplace. It was a place I loved and where I was so happy. As best I remember, the balance tipped as I headed home from our works' badminton club.

I remember at the time being somewhat exuberant. Mum and Dad were watching the television. Staring into the screen, the thought entered my mind that God was going to reward me for being good. I needed to escape. The next thing I knew I was in the back of an ambulance, heading for the local hospital's psychiatric ward. My vague memory was that it was evening time, and the ward was dark when we arrived. There was a faint light by a room. I later learnt that the room was the sister's office. The next memory was that a man appeared. I thought I had met with Jesus and passed out. We later laughed about this, as he became part of my life's journey. It has been a long time before I have been brave enough to share the thoughts that went through my mind at the time. They were part of an inner world that had been locked away inside. No-one was going to get a look in.

I woke up the next day in a hospital bed. It was a long ward, typical of its time. The closer you were to the sister's office, the more attention you needed. The further away, the nearer you were to being discharged. No surprise that I was close to the sister's office for a week or two. The only activity each day was to make your bed. At that time, I was incapable of doing anything else. The expression "hospital corners" may be familiar to some of you. In my circle, everyone knew what a hospital corner was, and the correct way to make a bed. What a blessing when duvets came into being! The days in hospital were long, seemingly endless. I could no longer communicate. What on earth had happened? With hindsight, a breakdown had been building up for some time. My body chemistry had really taken a big hit and eventually did what you might expect – shut down. I couldn't think or engage in a conversation with anyone. It was like being locked in a prison and frustrating beyond words. The only thought I had at the time was that there was something wrong with me, a thought I expressed to my nan when she came to visit me in hospital. To this day, I clearly remember Nan approaching my bedside, wearing a long coat, neat straw hat and handbag over her arm. As nan approached, my heart sank like a lead balloon. With a puzzled and concerned look on her face, Nan asked the question: "Oh dear Jean, what are you doing here?" My response was that I didn't know. All I could say was "Nan, there is something wrong with me." For someone who had been so full of life, this was a truly frightening experience. I had no idea what had happened, other than that something had gone wrong.

Before writing this next paragraph, I want to state that I am extremely grateful for the care I was given by the medical and nursing profession during my time in hospital and subsequent treatments I received. No-one really knows what is going on in a person's mind, what has impacted them negatively – often the person themself doesn't know. It has ultimately been my faith and the love and support of others that has finally seen me through.

My hospital stay lasted for months. Different medications were tried, all without success. I was comforted by one patient on the ward who, like me, clearly loved life. A bubbly personality, this lovely lady explained that she was treated for "manic depression" and what it was all about. Whatever has gone wrong, there is treatment. That was helpful. There was one other patient on the ward who was also bright and cheerful. Having shared that she had an addiction to alcohol, this patient was being given a short course of treatment that might help reverse her addiction. Apart from those two lovely ladies, life on the ward was somewhat depressing. I was given a series of tests, including an EEG (Electroencephalogram) testing for brain activity. The outcome ... thankfully, there was brain activity.

With little or no sign of the depression lifting, I was offered a course of six treatments of ECT (Electroconvulsive Therapy). I didn't relish the thought, however it seemed the only option, so I agreed to have the treatment. In my case, ECT was unsuccessful, and the way forward was to continue with anti-depressant medication. I was eventually discharged from hospital with the expectation that the depression/low mood would eventually lift, and that life would return to normal. It didn't — for a long time. The word "depression" can mean lots of different things to different people. I understood that a medical description of depression could include feelings of hopelessness, low self-esteem, finding no pleasure in life and "low mood." The reality was that my capacity to think, feel and interact had gone. I just felt dead inside, like a zombie. I could function mechanically, however, the person I was had somehow become trapped inside.

Thankfully, my employer had been incredibly kind. My job was kept open. I was allowed time to adjust to being home from hospital and was then gradually phased back into the workplace. Life wasn't as it had been before. I am thankful for the skills I had learnt at college and that those skills kicked back in, the kindness of my employer, including my boss. Everyone at work was both kind and assuring on my return. My work colleagues had always been like family to me, and it was great to be back with them again. A positive note here was that the other medications I had been taking before I became unwell, had also gone. It was as if that episode in my life hadn't happened, as some degree of normality was restored. In their place I took an anti-depressant on a daily basis. It didn't seem to make any difference. My head just felt a bit wooden inside. It felt a bit like a workshop that had been abandoned. I was assured that one day it would all clear. To be honest, although at a level there was a degree of normality, life for me wasn't how I wanted it to be or how I wanted to live out my life. The weeks and months ticked by. They were miserable years and I lived for the sake of others. There was no joy on the inside and an ache that I had not been born this way. I had no intention of ending my life in this state of mind. I had no solution, other than to press on and be thankful for the degree of routine that had returned to my life.

The one significant blot on the horizon was that socially my confidence had gone. The workplace was safe and familiar. What about the world outside? A possible solution to the problem came in an unexpected way, via yet another friend of my mum's. This lady had once worked as a barmaid. The suggestion was that I might consider applying for a job as a barmaid. This would give me a social life. There would be a bar between me and the customers, yet I might learn to interact socially again. I took her advice, and again turned to the infamous "Liverpool Echo." A part-time evening job was advertised. I applied and was offered the job. I left home on my first night, somewhat apprehensive. I was not the person I had been. Stepping out into a different world was a bit of an ordeal, however, all went reasonably well. Whilst not solving the problem, I slowly gained confidence socially.

A door opened for me to move on to another pub, where I met someone who would become a life-long friend, so much so that I was very much accepted into her family. Life became brighter. Maureen and I would regularly meet her mum on Saturday mornings in Ormskirk. Saturdays were market day. The three of us would have coffee together, then Maureen and I would go off in search of bargains. We usually managed to find our bargain, often something to wear that night as we took to our roles as barmaids.

In the middle of ploughing my way through the difficult challenges life had presented, disaster struck again. Maureen's mum became unwell. After a series of investigations, the diagnosis was oesophageal cancer. At the time, this was a relatively new form of cancer with the only form of treatment likely to be exploratory. Initially, Maureen's mum was admitted to a cancer hospital for treatment. I would regularly visit and would be met with a lovely smile and with no thought for herself, Maureen's mum would give me a run-down of her concern for each of the patients on the ward. On one such visit I was shown the marks where Maureen senior would be receiving radiotherapy. After each visit, Maureen's mum would always end our conversation with the words "God is good." This presented a significant challenge for me and caused me to recall what had been a particular challenge in my life.

When I was just seventeen years of age, my maternal grandfather had become unwell. "Pop" as he was known to us, had served in the regular army in India for twenty-five years. It was a time we knew he had thoroughly enjoyed, which at the same time had left him with a bad chest. Pop's chest was particularly bad on this occasion and Mum sent for our doctor. The upshot was that my grandfather needed to be hospitalised. To this day I remember so clearly the moment the ambulance arrived and my grandfather being stretchered out. I ran down to church as fast as I could, got on my knees, and asked God to make my grandfather better. By the time I arrived home, I was met with the heartbreaking news that my grandfather had died. To me, he had been invincible. Why had God not answered a simple prayer? The following Sunday, I went to church. The joy, enthusiasm and expectation I had had each Sunday had gone out the window. Soon after Pop's death, we moved home and relocated to Aintree. My friends and I had all moved on, myself to commercial college, my friends to teacher training college/university. I didn't know anyone from the local church with the result that I slowly drifted. My life was on hold.

So, here was a challenge. My friend's mum was seriously ill, radiotherapy hadn't worked and following further consultation, a door opened for what was in fact exploratory surgery. There was no guaranteed outcome. For Maureen senior this was a win-win situation. Were surgery successful, life would go on. Were it unsuccessful, Maureen knew that she would be going home to her Lord and Saviour, hopefully with the surgeon learning something that would help the next patient. Whilst the surgery had been successful, Maureen senior only survived the operation by a few weeks.

This very sad time became an unexpected turning point in my life. With my closeness to the family, I was invited to the requiem mass. As the coffin was brought into the church, the young choir began singing "Morning has broken." My heart lifted. A light went on. For my grandfather, death had not been the end, rather he had gone on into a "new day." Where was this to take me? How would this help me? Would I no longer need to take medication? Enter the Good Samaritan.

The upshot of this rather sad time was that my heart was stirred by Maureen senior's faith. At what must have been a difficult time, both Maureen and Maureen senior had a very clear faith and a confidence in God, no matter what was going on around them. I was really impressed. I had spent lots of time with the family. Apart from spending time with Maureen, Maureen senior and I met for coffee on Saturday mornings. Their faith in God truly was the bedrock of their lives. My journey through life had been somewhat different. I had a very simple faith. My nan had painted such a good picture of a loving God who had created the wonderful world we lived in. Death had never featured in the equation for me. I had just skipped happily through life.

I now had a challenge and had to do some thinking. Could this be a part of the mist clearing, my having a different perspective on life? Even as a young person, I had attended family funerals. It was part of our family tradition for younger members of the family to be included at family funerals. It had simply been a way of life. The death of my grandfather had been completely different. Pop really had been the patriarch of the family. There was something almost ethereal about him – almost untouchable. He was someone I greatly admired. I felt safe as long as he was around. He was a man of few words, each one counted. When my brother and I played out, Pop would be standing in the doorway, watching out for us. Woe betide anyone who might try to harm us. With his death, that anchor, that security had gone.

I knew I needed to find my way back to church again. Those seeds of faith sown by my nan were coming to life again. The horizon was looking a little brighter. And another unexpected blessing came my way. At this time, my parents had a small sweetshop/news agency. One of the ladies who helped in the shop was Edie, another person who became a dear friend. Edie, a widow of many years, was a member of the local Anglican church. This was in fact the church where my parents were married and where my brother and I had been christened. Sharing with Edie what had happened at the requiem mass, I also shared that I had many unanswered questions about my faith, and yet I wanted to go back to church again. Edie had two sons, the eldest of whom was in ministry in London. "Next time Freddie is home," Edie said, "I'll ask him to pop over and have a coffee with you." which Edie did.

Enter the Good Samaritan. I will never underestimate the value of a conversation over a cup of coffee. Freddie (or more correctly Father Freddie, an Anglican priest) spent time with me, patiently listening. Then came his response to my uncertainties. "Don't be concerned," said dear Freddie, "about what you don't understand. The fact that you want to start going back to church again is a sign that the Lord is calling you back into the fold." What kind and encouraging words they were. Freddie then described God's love to me. "It's like this," said Freddie "when you are at the bottom of a mountain, you look to the top, and you see a tiny flower. The closer you get, the more beautiful the flower becomes. God's love is like that. From a distance, we get a glimpse, a faint picture of what He is like. The more you climb, the nearer you get, the more real becomes the beauty of God's love."

With that encouragement, Freddie left. How kind to spare me the time when he was home from London on a short visit and had family to spend time with. Edie subsequently called for me each Sunday. Freddie and I became lifelong friends. The journey to understanding, to inner healing, had begun. What had come to be known as "depression" didn't go away; however, seeds of faith that had been sown that day eventually bore fruit in my life and "depression" became a thing of the past.

Battles lay ahead. Attending church each week, I was conscious that I didn't have the freedom that other members of the congregation had. I persevered. Battles followed, as did another period of hospitalisation and by this time I had been diagnosed as having "manic depression" as it was then called (nowadays more kindly known as "bipolar disorder"). A blessing at this time was the conviction deep down that I had not been born with this "illness" and I had a determination in my heart that it wouldn't defeat me. Over time, I was able to identify a pattern. I could literally feel the chemical balance in my body going, my body chemistry would alter, my persona would change from being happy and outgoing into dark feelings and a fearful trip down memory lane. This would be completely debilitating and keep me out of action for weeks at a time. I would hit the depths slowly. With medication my body chemistry would re-balance and life would resume "as normal" (or rather, I would surface from the dark memories of the past). Once chemical balance was restored, so also would my focus change. I would become positive and forward-looking and medication would be discontinued.

## JEAN DOBSON

## CHAPTER 5
# LONDON, LIGHT, DREAMS AND VISIONS

I had come to terms with life as it was shaping up. Alongside times of debilitating thoughts and feelings, there were times when life was good, mostly because of my ability to work. To this day, I am thankful for the basic skills I had acquired and that despite hiccups along the way, I was able to earn a living. I just loved the challenging and interesting world of the workplace; my happy place.

An unusual opportunity presented itself, after one such bout of what I understood to be a clinical depression. Once I surfaced again, I saw an advert in a national newspaper for a secretarial post in London. It seemed quite interesting and I had always found London fascinating. I applied for the job and to my surprise was invited to London for an interview. At this point, my dear friend Edie offered to travel to London with me, which would give her the opportunity to spend time with her son Freddie. The interview over, Edie and I were invited over to the presbytery for refreshments with Freddie before taking the train back home to Liverpool. While we were chatting, the phone rang and to my surprise I was offered the job. I put the phone down and exclaimed, "Oh dear! Where am I going to live?" I hadn't thought that far ahead. My dear friend Freddie came to the rescue: "I might be able to help. I'll give one of my parishioners a ring." It just so happened that one of Freddie's parishioners was shortly to have a vacancy for a lodger in her home. We spoke on the phone and Cicely invited me to be her next lodger, suggesting Mum and Dad might accompany me on a visit to her home ahead of me taking up residency.

Mission accomplished: Mum and Dad enjoyed their day out. A throw-away comment from Dad later resonated in my journey to freedom. Dad was surprised that I had invited him to London to meet the lady who was to become my landlady. I don't really know what Dad's thoughts were at the time. Possibly, having learnt that Cicely was a retired Shakespearean actress, the thought might have been daunting? Whilst I had been introduced to Shakespeare at senior school, it may have been a far cry away from Dad's early years and life experience. There had been no one in our family who had connections with a "real-life" actress. Cicely certainly had a rather tasteful home in the Finchley area of London, a shortish walk away from Hampstead Heath. Yet there were no sides to this remarkable and interesting lady, who had driven ambulances in Chester during the second world war.

We became good friends, sharing our evening meals together. In between acting parts, Cicely had been friends with a lady who had her own restaurant and had written cookery books. How blessed was I? Cicely was a fabulous cook. All this, and heaven too, I thought. A member of the congregation of St Mary's, Bourne Street, Cicely would drive me to church each Sunday. What an experience that was. I was amazed at this lady's driving skills as we would wind in and out of traffic in this vast city of London. Cicely was also a lay reader at the church. One particular Sunday morning comes to mind. It was the

Sunday when Cicely read from the book of Ezekiel and the account of the valley of dry bones. Boy did that scripture come to life!

Through links with St Mary's, I discovered that there was an Anglican church not too far from my workplace that held healing meetings each month. Could this be the real reason I was in London? I certainly knew that there was something wrong. Medication kept me on an even keel, yet the freedom I had once known had gone.

I decided to go along to one of the healing services. I can remember little of the service up to the point where members of the congregation were invited to go forward to have hands laid on for healing. My turn came. No-one could have been prepared for what then followed. As hands were laid on me, a well of pain on the inside broke out on the surface and I cried out, almost screamed out (as I was later told) uncontrollably. The team, I subsequently learnt, were so concerned, they sent for the aid of another minister, who was experienced in deliverance ministry.

I was taken separately to a private chapel for further prayer ministry. The minister was kind and reassuring. As he prayed for me, the most awful painful memories began to surface, one by one. I had been sexually abused as a child. What was incredibly weird was the fact that the occasions of abuse all happened at significant times in my life. The first incident took place, in a setting we now know to be common, within the family. The abuser was a widower who became a relative; a relative who had in later life married a maiden aunt. The abuser, as you might expect, asked me not to share with anyone what had taken place. By agreeing to his request, I had unknowingly locked myself into a prison, spoken promise, not to let anyone into our "little secret." I entered a silent world, unknown to anyone else.

The second abuse came as I learnt that I had passed my eleven plus exam. I had been given money by family and immediately headed off to what we knew as "the corner shop" to buy sweets to share with everyone. En route home, a man stopped me and asked me the way to a street in the area. Before I knew what had happened, he had walked me down an entry, I was pinned against a wall and the abuse took place. I screamed out in horror, and thankfully the man ran way. A neighbour came to my aid, the police were sent for, and I found myself in the back of a police van, scouring the neighbourhood. It was no surprise to learn that the offender had scarpered and was nowhere to be seen.

Several further events happened, all as I began to grow from childhood into womanhood. I was abused by a man who sat next to me on the school bus, as I was on my way to senior school. I was terrified. I went cold inside. Eventually I told my nan what had happened to me and my parents contacted the school. It just so happened that the same man was also assaulting another pupil from the same school as me and on the same bus route. Private detectives were assigned to the case. The offender was caught and charged with the offences. Not only was the ordeal terrifying, equally terrifying was the need for my friend and I to be in court, should the offender not plead guilty. It was horrifying seeing the man again. Thankfully, the culprit pleaded guilty and we weren't required to give evidence. A subsequent attack took place one winter night, as I headed off to youth club. Out of nowhere a man came up and attacked me from behind. The result for me was terrifying winter nights, both leaving for and returning from youth club. My mum recalled hearing my footsteps as I ran up our road as fast as I could during those winter months, terrified that another abuser might appear out of nowhere. The culmination of this abuse ended in my being raped in my early twenties. They were all horrifying experiences and both the pain and memory had been locked inside. I had almost been de-humanised as a child, a teenager and a woman. The ability to be able to unburden myself and share these experiences with someone who had the compassion to listen and the wisdom how to pray began part of the healing journey into freedom.

My time in London came to an end. I returned home to Liverpool and whilst I had received a measure of freedom, I knew that there were more issues to be dealt with. I just didn't know how or when. I took up a secretarial appointment at our local hospital, and by way of relaxation, joined the Liverpool Ramblers – introduced to them by yet another friend of mum's. The open spaces, the varied and beautiful landscape proved therapy of their own. On one such day, we walked the Long Mynd in Derbyshire. It was another memorable day and a stepping stone to freedom. It was an autumn day, the weather was perfect for walking, and from the top of the Long Mynd there were beautiful views. On our descent down, we were rewarded with a farmhouse tea. I can recall the lovely home-made scones, lemon drizzle cake and welcome cups of tea. Refreshed, we headed for home.

By this time, I had my own flat. Overcoming the fears that had surrounded me from the various times of abuse, I had verses of scripture in every room of my flat. Only as I write do I realise how the fear of man had become a snare. No matter what the past had held, I was holding on to God's word to see me through into my future. With work the next day, I had a long soak in the bath and headed off to bed, where I had the strangest dream ever. I can see it now, as clear as day. I saw myself in a short wedding dress, at a side altar. I wanted to see more. What was going to happen next? The dream came and went. It all made sense a little further down the road. For me to even have a dream about being married was in itself weird. I had considered marriage to be for wimps and for people who couldn't stand on their own two feet. How wrong was I on that count.

I headed off to work on the Monday morning, giving no more thought to the dream, with my focus on what the working week would hold for me. And, to my surprise, an unusual encounter one weekend. On Saturday mornings I would take my washing to our local launderette. On one morning in particular I noticed a rather handsome man seated to my right. Engrossed in my morning read, there was a sudden tap on my newspaper by an older lady, wearing a headscarf and looking somewhat dishevelled. The reason for the tap? The lady was asking for money. I'd no idea what the cause was, but just someone in need of money. The handsome gentleman seated nearby helped the lady out of the launderette and a conversation opened up between us, mainly around how sad it was that someone could be so needy as to drop into a launderette to ask for money. The conversation ended as one wash finished and this knight in shining armour left the launderette.

A few weeks later, and nearing Christmas, I was heading home after a shopping expedition into Liverpool. As the bus I was on neared what is known as "The Black Bull" stop, I noticed someone on a nearby corner selling wrapping paper. An item I had forgotten. I jumped off the bus to make my purchase, and who should I bump into, none other than the gentleman from the launderette. Surprised at meeting up again, our conversation from the launderette continued as we walked along, as it happened, both walking in the same direction. It turned out that our families had been neighbours when we were both younger. For whatever reason, our paths hadn't crossed until now. On reaching my road, Norman asked for my phone number. A phone call followed and a few days later, we agreed to go on a date. We ended up at an eating place in Liverpool known as "The Slaughter House" (so called because it had originally been located near to what was Liverpool's abattoir, where pub food was served and where Norman that night shared his life story). With a disastrous and disappointing time in America behind him, a family feud and a marriage which had ended in divorce, Norman had turned to God for help. At his mum's invitation, Norman attended a service at her local church where a visiting speaker was sharing his experiences of life as a missionary in South Africa. Having lived in South Africa himself, Norman was drawn to that evening to hear the speaker. To everyone's surprise, Norman gave his life to Jesus that night and was about to be baptised as an adult. How interesting was this! I knew nothing of adult baptism and was intrigued by this step of faith that Norman was about to take. It really appealed to me. Although I had been christened and confirmed in the Church of England, I knew nothing of adult baptism. The idea really appealed to me. Despite having received prayer in London from the abuse I had suffered, I still felt unclean. I had forgiven my abusers yet felt unclean. Evidence of the damage that had been done, still remained. Maybe being baptised, immersed in water, would bring the cleansing which seemed to escape me.

I met with Norman's minister and his lovely mum, at a Sunday evening service. There was an immediate bond between us. I explained my situation to the pastor, who agreed that I too could be included in the baptismal service. That afternoon, I prayed ahead of my baptism, in my heart I hoped that I would be cleansed of all that I had been exposed to over the years. I was drawn to a particular passage of scripture in the book of Malachi, which read:

> *"But for you who fear my name, the Sun of Righteousness will rise with healing in his wings"* (Malachi 4:2).

Alongside the scripture was a simple, stick like drawing, of the sun rising and bringing healing. I knew instantly that healing would come my way. It wasn't instant.

Adult baptism was a fabulous experience, both for Norman and me. By this time we had become engaged and were married four months later. Then began the next and significant journey into freedom. As an adult, coming to faith, Norman read the New Testament scriptures and believed that in God anything was possible. In the short three and a half years that we were married, the Lord certainly did some amazing things, restoring everything that Norman had lost over the previous years of his life. Norman became a member of a local branch of the "Full

Gospel Businessman's Fellowship International" or "FGBMFI" as it was known locally. This is a Christian evangelistic ministry founded by a man by the name of Demos Shakarian, a Californian rancher. The group met monthly for prayer and had monthly outreach dinner meetings, with a view to reaching businessmen with the good news of Jesus.

At some of these meetings, ladies were invited. It was at one of these meetings that I had the most amazing experience and a significant milestone on my journey through to freedom. The guest speaker at this particular event was a man by the name of Steve Ryder. Steve and his family had re-located from Yorkshire to Australia when Steve was in his teens. Steve had missed all his friends from home, got involved in a gang from Australia and at one point found himself in solitary confinement in a prison in Australia. The gang had attempted armed robbery on a bank. Fast forward, Steve became a follower of Jesus and a world-wide evangelist. As Steve shared his testimony, there was an invitation for people to give their lives to Jesus or to be baptised in the Holy Spirit. This had been a real stumbling block for me. Having had my formative years in the Church of England, I had no real understanding of the person of the Holy Spirit and His role as part of the Trinity. I sat at our table, feeling a little uncomfortable, weighing up what Steve had shared. Then, without question of doubt, I saw Jesus clearly calling me forward. On invitation, I stepped forward with other guests that evening for hands to be laid on me and to be baptised in the Holy Spirit. Another step forward into freedom. God took hold of a woman who had been battered and bruised by life and turned her whole life around. The person of the Holy Spirit gave me a confidence I had never known and opened up scriptures to me. I had previously read my Bible out of duty. It became a joy. Day by day I learnt that the Creator of the whole universe would speak to me through scripture. What joy!

The next three years were something like a whirlwind. Our home became like a ministry centre, where we regularly prayed for those in need. Life was a breeze. We led both of our dads to the Lord. Then a hiccup! By trade, Norman was a sheet-metal worker. At a particular time, the men with whom Norman was working were becoming ill. We regularly prayed for them all. Eventually sickness hit Norman. Long story short, after a wonderful holiday in Northern Spain, we met up with two Spanish families, who had been long-time friends of Norman. At this point, Norman became seriously unwell and we returned to England. Norman was hospitalised and after several months, his earthly journey came to an end, and he made his journey heavenward. The last part of healing in Norman's life was reconciliation with his brother. They had had a major fall-out whilst Norman was in America, which hadn't healed. Just four days before Norman breathed his last, his brother arrived from America and thankfully reconciliation took place.

I sat at Norman's bedside, just five days before he died. Norman was clearly unwell. We both trusted the Lord. In a quiet moment, I heard the still small voice of God speaking to me: "Will you still love Me if I take him?" was the question. My reply: "I have no choice, Lord." At that moment, strange though it may seem, I had such a sense of peace and was even able to read from scripture at Norman's funeral. Post-funeral came the real turning point in my life. As you might expect, Emily, Norman's mum was devastated at his passing – he was just forty-seven years of age. Emily was a member of one of the church's house groups. It was suggested that I might join that group and that we might both be a support to each other in our time of grief. The house group leader was Philip, to whom I later became engaged and to whom I have been happily married for these last thirty-four years.

In bringing this chapter to a close, I am returning to a dream I had just prior to meeting Norman and which I have already shared. The dream was of myself at a side altar. I saw myself in the dress I wore at my wedding to Norman, and as I have previously shared, the dream came to a quick end. There was nothing to the dream other than that the wedding wouldn't be straight forward. I was reminded of the dream one day as I went out for a walk with my mother-in-law, distraught at the loss of her younger son at so young an age. I shared the dream with her. There were complications around my marriage to Norman in that, when we met, he was a divorced man. I was worshipping in an Anglican church where a divorced person wasn't allowed to re-marry. My minister expressed concern at the step I was about to take. At the church which Norman attended, a Pentecostal church, little was known about him, even less about me and they felt unable to marry us. The upshot was that after prayer, my minister agreed to ask God's blessing on our marriage. We married at a registry office in Liverpool. The marriage was blessed by the minister at my local church. It was a big step for the vicar and I will ever be thankful to him for his obedience to God. Long story short, Norman had married his first wife against his father's wishes. The marriage had ended in failure. There were broken hearts all round. God had put it all right within just the few years we were married.

Why do I write this? Quite simply, when dark thoughts and feelings can cloud our minds, there is nothing that will stop God reaching out to us. When mentally I couldn't always make sense of things, when vision was clouded, the Lord graciously spoke to me through dreams and visions. There is nothing that will stop Him in his efforts to reach out to us and set us free from those things that would hinder our walk through this life.

## CHAPTER 6
# MINISTRY, FORMISSION, FREEDOM IN SIGHT

For someone who had thought that marriage was for wimps I began to realise that friendship, commitment and partnership had all added something quite unexpected and rich to my life's experience. It was quite different to my parents' experience of married life. The outbreak of World War Two had temporarily changed the landscape. Within weeks of being married, Dad had been flown out to India, Mum stayed at home looking after Nan and Pop. My parents were apart for three and a half years. The only communication was by letter. Whilst Dad was serving in the RAF all those thousands of miles away, back home Mum was living through the constant bombing of Liverpool and even closer to home, the attempted bombing of two railway lines in walking distance from the family home.

After being widowed, I began reading "Song of Solomon" by Watchman Nee. At the same time Phil was reading the same story from the book of the same name in the Bible. We became good friends, and before too long were engaged to be married.

Marriage to Phil saw life take on a whole new turn. I was serving in the NHS, Phil was serving in the City Council and was at the same time holding a leading role in our local church. Not long after we were married, an opportunity came for us to be part of a church plant in

Liverpool. The pastor who established the church plant had come from a place called Bedworth, in Coventry and as a result of links Phil had with him at the time, was the man who married us.

What an amazing experience we had as we became part of the city centre church plant, based just on the edge of what is known as China Town. This was a Pentecostal church, vibrant, energetic and outward-looking. During our time there, we became part of the wider leadership. It was a time where my faith began to grow as did my prayer life. The development of my prayer life is significant to my story and something which I will come back to.

The point came when Phil had the opportunity to take early retirement and work full-time at church, initially as Personal Assistant to the senior minister at the city centre church plant, which grew in numbers to around four hundred people at its peak. We regularly hosted students for lunch on Sundays, were active members of a house group and in addition to my full-time job did some part-time work with Phil to support our income. At that point in time, there were no funds to pay a Personal Assistant. The inevitable happened and cycles of "depression" would set in. They were quite scary, although, in a way, I had become used to them. I could feel the chemistry in my body change and dark and debilitating thoughts would see me out of activity for several weeks. Eventually, with medication, balance would be restored and I would be back on my feet again.

The time came for our founding pastor to move on, and a door of opportunity presented itself for Phil to go into full-time ministry. By this time, Phil had undergone ministerial training with the Assemblies of God and was a fully accredited minister. A friend in ministry was returning to America and he suggested Phil might be considered to take over the pastorate, which eventually was the case. We found ourselves in Toxteth, leading a small Assemblies of God church, in an area surrounded by men's hostels, with a woman's hostel immediately opposite the church building. This was an absolute godsend. Phil was fulfilled in his ministry and I loved working alongside him, as best I could, still serving full-time in the NHS.

At this point, you might wonder what on earth this has to do with finding freedom. Here, I hope is an encouragement. Whilst there is life, there is hope; with hope, we can keep going. The reality for me was that there was so much to unpack in my life and so much that had been hidden away. I wouldn't have coped if it had all been unpacked at once. If hidden to me, how could any healthcare professional have any greater success in uncovering what lay behind the happy exterior. The answers lie within us and bit by bit the mystery behind dark thoughts and feelings will unfold. I did at one time feel really cheated. Yet another friend of the family had said to Dad: "When they find out what is troubling Jean, she will be fine." The number of times those words came to mind, the number of times! No conversation ever took place about what was troubling me. I would become more discouraged. At least medication restored the balance. I had learnt to live with life as it was and would on occasions recall to mind the words of the psychiatrist who treated me when in hospital and for whom I had the greatest respect. "At least it won't kill you," he said. Those words sparked something off inside me, apart from the obvious. Again, something I will refer to a little later on. Strange though it may seem, I knew he was right, and I am sure he felt safe enough to share that thought with me. Deep down inside I knew that one day life would change and what, on occasions, seemed a great weight weighing down on my mind would go.

What I realised at this time was the love I had for people, more deeply God's love for people and especially those who were so much in need of help and support. We set up free meals for our homeless community, serving a hot meal on Wednesdays, and a full English breakfast on Saturday mornings. I can't tell you how much joy this brought. With a team of supporters, we would serve up to one hundred breakfasts each Saturday morning. There was something hidden to my mind at the back of this, which I will explain later. I was drawn to the plight of the homeless, the situations that had led them to hostel living and to even begging on the streets of Liverpool. It was the city where I was born and bred. Situations happen in our lives which can all be signposts, pointing us to freedom.

Realising that our time in Toxteth was coming to an end and that we needed to hand over the leadership to the next person, we headed off to a Christian retreat in Spain, where the prompting to write first came. Not long before, I had had a dream, a picture of "broken people": outwardly with happy faces, yet with a hidden inner brokenness. It was a reminder, too, of a Christmas card I had been drawn to at one time. The picture on the front of the card was of a rather jolly Father Christmas with a long white beard, wearing gold-rimmed round spectacles and holding in his lap an Edwardian style soldier and doll.

I had had a third dream, which was all part of the same picture. The dream was of an operating theatre, the surgeon had white hair, wore a white coat, and also wore gold-rimmed round spectacles. The surgeon in the picture was God, who wanted to heal people and mend broken lives.

We had met a couple who had come to help us in our ministry to the homeless. This couple took over the leadership of our church for us as we headed off to southern Spain and the prompting to write grew. Day by day, as we sat on our terrace, over breakfast I would get ideas for chapter headings for a book, then ideas as to what each chapter might contain. It was all rather surreal.

We came home from our retreat and there was a clear call for us to lay down our ministry. The couple who had stood in for us were our clear successors. We approached our oversight, who were in clear agreement, and the handover of leadership took place. Then came the turning point, which truly opened the door to my freedom. How did this move see a door open? As ever, my journey has been one of surprises. I have always loved surprises, as well as surprising others. This next step became another and yet significant step in my journey to freedom.

We stayed on for a short while in Toxteth to hand over our leadership to this couple. The husband had separately embarked on a course of ministry training through a college known as ForMission College. The college trains and equips leaders for mission within their own communities, particularly across Europe and the UK. The mission field at home had changed – we needed a different understanding and a clearer vision of home mission for today. Encouraged by this leader's enthusiasm, my husband Phil also applied for a place on the degree course and his application was successful. Phil was so enthusiastic by what he was learning at college as he embarked on his first six months of teaching, that in a throw-away comment from me, I found myself also applying for a place on the three-year degree course. How amazing and unexpected that was!

It was in the second year of college that a real breakthrough came, and in, as ever, an unexpected way. I remember being in class when, as had previously been the case for me, I heard that still small voice of God: "You didn't think you could do this, did you?" "Absolutely not," was my response. My mind immediately went back to the time I came out from a school assembly and was drawn to the school noticeboard. At that time, my thoughts had been all over the place. I had wanted to go on to teacher training, yet I wasn't sure how well I would do, nor how my parents would foot the bill. For whatever reason, at the back of my mind was the thought that it was more important that my younger brother should have the opportunity of further education.

After all, males were to be the bread winners (or so I had thought at the time). I had eliminated myself from a career in teaching and from any possibility of higher education. How amazing – here I was, in a place I thought I would never be, at a college of higher education, studying for an honours degree in Theology and Mission. My thoughts all those years ago were to train to be a P.E. teacher. How my life, my aspirations and my understanding had changed. And what an amazing door God had opened for me, taking me in a completely different direction. It was a very different direction to where I had thought my life might lead all those years ago.

This was followed by yet another incredible and unexpected door opening to me. You've probably picked up by now that the word "unexpected" crops up a number of times during the course of this book. I share this to encourage you, the reader, to expect the unexpected. We can think we have got everything all sorted; we've eliminated ourselves from achieving things for a variety of different reasons – life couldn't be any different. We find ourselves living within our own set limitations, without even realising it. Then there is God. As unexpectedly as life can throw you a googly, so can God present you with a solution.

After one of our college tutorials, an unexpected conversation opened with one of our tutors around abuse. I can't remember exactly how the subject arose, other than our tutor shared that he himself had come from a background where there had been sexual abuse within the family. Outside of college, he was doing a series of podcasts and asked if he could interview me for a podcast he was doing on sexual abuse. With my husband's OK, we agreed to meet up for an interview to be recorded.

As the interview got under way I had an absolute lightbulb moment, as a result of a throw-away comment from my tutor. We arrived at the point where I shared about a man sitting next to me on the bus, heading for senior school, when this particular abuse took place. The tutor who interviewed me made this remark: "So this is fairly normal?" You are sitting on a bus, heading for school, a man sits next to you, and begins to abuse you.

This is normal?" This was an electric shock moment—this was a life changer. For the first time in my life, I realised that what had been happening to me hadn't been "normal." This was the moment when I began to think for myself. College life had been life-enhancing. This one moment in time was life-changing. The road to freedom was beginning to open.

Had what had been happening to me really been normal? How many of us, along life's way, just accept things that happen to us as being "part of life." For sure it isn't, and a long way from what God intends for our lives. That question, for me, was such a life changer. So much of what had happened to me along life's way had been "life." This is what life throws at you. Stiff upper lip, keep your chin up, get on with life and get on with it.

This truly was a life-changing moment and the moment that set me on the road to freedom. I was born into a home that was what I understood to be "Church of England." That for me had translated into meaning that we were a Christian family. It was something of a shock to realise that we weren't. This was something I had never questioned until I started attending church regularly and was keen to understand more of the Christian faith. Jesus for sure was a great role model. What the family said was what went. I was never allowed to question at home, although there were doubts that crept in and which eventually caused me to leave home. The family were never part of a church community although I knew that my grandmother had been part of a local church until the day her son died prematurely at the age of nineteen. The order of life was what it was until that college tutor, by the very nature of his question, "So this is normal?" began the journey of my questioning what in fact "was normal." If black was said to be white, white it was.

I was raised in a family where there was a strong patriarchal structure, although there were times when it would seem, on reflection, that women had more of a say. Without question of doubt, "children were to be seen, not to be heard." This had continued, quite surprisingly, into my adult life. Whilst I had grown to be an adult, yet I had been treated as a child. I am confident that growth in the home had been hampered unintentionally. The blessing had been that my working life had enabled me to grow, serving in a variety of roles as a secretary/PA/Admin Assistant to some very senior managers, certainly stretching me intellectually and without me realising at the time.

The main bone of contention and the reason I left home in my mid-thirties was my faith and Mum's opposition in particular to my times of prayer. I couldn't make sense of it at the time. There was a point when Mum would say of my faith: "That's OK for you, just don't bring it home here." I had no understanding why, other than that it was a difficult subject. As my faith grew, and in particular my prayer life, it became impossible for me to stay at home. Mum was concerned that I might develop "religious mania." All came to light in rather sad circumstances. My brother who was married with two sons suddenly became unwell. After a series of tests my brother was eventually hospitalised and diagnosed as having an incurable form of cancer. My brother had always been full of fun, someone who had enjoyed life to the full, had some good friends, had done well at work and eventually gained a professional qualification. Whilst there was the inevitable rivalry in our early years, we grew up to be very close and were always there for each other.

The day came when we visited my brother in hospital and were given the sad news that he had at best just twelve months to live. Colin asked me would I share the diagnosis with Mum. It was the hardest thing I ever had to do. Mum, though small in height and build was, like her father, very strong in character. As I shared the news with her, she burst into tears and shared a secret fear that had been locked inside all these years. That was the only time in my life I ever saw her cry. I was shocked to the core. On her side of the family, there had been a pattern of young males dying prematurely, very close to home. Of course, there was her brother who had died at nineteen years of age. Mum shared with me that from the day that Colin had been born, there had been a fear, locked away inside, that one day something would happen to my brother and that she would lose him prematurely. There were other fears around Mum's understanding of who God was. A picture of God, which some people have had, of the angry God of the Old Testament. My journey had led me to get to know God in a much different way – a loving, kind, forgiving and gracious Creator, who loves His creation, and the reason His son died for us. Mum, I am sure, is not the only person to have had that image of God: cold, angry, harsh, unforgiving.

We supported Mum and my brother as best we could during the difficult months which ensued. The day came when my brother's life was coming to an end. I was called to his bedside and had the privilege of leading him to the Lord. Mum was able to visit a few hours later, my brother was still with us, and thankfully they both had some precious moments together. Phil took Mum home, my brother's two closest friends visited him and Phil and I were alone with Colin as he passed away, peacefully, just minutes into what turned out to be our wedding anniversary. We went straight to be with Mum. We looked after her as best we could, however Mum never recovered from the loss, began visibly to shrink before our eyes and passed on herself just eight months later.

I was devastated by the loss. I had hoped for a different outcome. At the very least they had made their peace with God. I wept uncontrollably at Mum's funeral and at the time I didn't know why. All will come together as the door to freedom opens – the door to freedom and finding the person hidden within.

JEAN DOBSON

## CHAPTER 7
# THE MENTAL MAZE, GIANTS DEFEATED

From weeping uncontrollably at Mum's funeral to walking through the mental maze to a place of freedom! How on earth did that take place? What does the word "maze" conjure up in your mind? The first thing that comes to my mind is the story of 'Alice in Wonderland' and the "Queen's Maze" which Alice had to navigate. At any point in time, as Alice wound her way through the maze, card soldiers would pop up, to the cry of the queen, "Off with their heads!"

It was time for the journey through the mental maze to begin. It can be fraught with challenges and yet, we know for sure that a maze has an entrance point and a destination, a centre point. Like the maze in 'Alice in Wonderland' I am likening this to a large maze built of hedges, that in themselves can be intimidating. The hardest part is taking the brave step to start the journey, with a determination to get to the centre point of the maze. The object of the journey for me was to discover where those debilitating thoughts and feelings had come from, how had they clouded my life and at the end, how would they go? The one thing that kept me going was the fact that I had not been born this way. I had had many happy years. How had these dark clouds set in? There had to be a reason. Equally, I was determined that at some point the sun would have to shine through. There had to be some logical explanation. I wasn't born that way, and I wouldn't end my life that way; and now to the journey through the mental maze.

What did I have to help me? Quite simply, a pathway. Hedges can seem large and intimidating, yet there is a path to walk through. To help me, I had the person of the Holy Spirit, daily reading scripture and the love and support of my husband and church family. There have been clues along the way, as there are through a maze. I'll start with where this chapter begins, the memory of crying uncontrollably at Mum's funeral. Mum's death was very sudden. From a fall on a Friday, to being hospitalised, by the Monday she had passed away. Phil and I were at her bedside from late Sunday evening to mid-morning the next day when her earthly journey came to an end. It was a shock to my system and yet a relief. Phil thankfully did most of the organising of her funeral and a dear friend in ministry took the service. Significantly for me, the service was held at the church where Phil and I were married, the place my nan had attended many years before, accompanied by Mum when she was very young. The church has had different denominations from when it was originally founded.

What brought the incredible outpouring of grief on the day of the funeral? It has taken me a long time to get there. I had wept for the sadness of her life. Outwardly she was a very capable housewife and mother who proved to be a good businesswoman when Mum and Dad went into business. What had been bottled up inside me had been the sadness of seeing how different life could have been for her if she had known Jesus so much earlier in her life. I had had flashbacks of the many times she would be angry, often around Sunday lunch when I guess pressure would be the greatest. My brother would head off to play football, I would head off to church and Mum would scurry around preparing the traditional Sunday lunch for both ourselves as a family and my grandparents. I would come home, enthusiastic from what I had learnt in church and would ask Dad questions. Whilst Dad was often able to offer some understanding, Mum would find this frustrating, suggesting that he had "lost his way in life" and more likely should have "gone in for the ministry." I hasten to add, Mum was not a bad person, however there were occasions when she could be very angry about something, which could be quite intimidating when I was younger. I had no idea how many of those moments I had stored away.

I also realised that underneath I had been very disappointed at what she had learnt about God that had been so different to my learning and understanding. I found it hard to make sense of why she had been so anti-God. The first giant fell as I realised over time that she hadn't been anti-God, just anti-church. How times change. From the church she attended as a young person, her understanding was that God would be offended if even a button was sown on a shirt on a Sunday. The only activity to be encouraged was Bible reading. Another misconception arose on Saturdays. Mum had been allowed to go to the local cinema on a Saturday with her brother and their cousin, for the Saturday matinee. There was one condition from her brother, that she didn't talk throughout the afternoon. Mum could manage that. What did concern her was a fear that someone from the church might see her going to the pictures. To this day, that is so alien to my understanding of God and the teaching I have received along life's way. How sad for her to have lived with that fear. How thankful I was that her life didn't end that way. I wept for the years she had lost. There had been many disappointments in life. Dad even referenced disappointment in his "father of the bride" speech at my marriage to Phil.

Alongside this came a second giant: one of loyalty. It was something I would pride myself in; I was a loyal person. Misplaced loyalty had caused me to be imprisoned by past negative experiences. Truth sets us free. Facing the impact those occasions had was key to being released from painful memories. I had misunderstood the meaning of loyalty. Nan was, to me, as near perfect as anyone could be. Gentle and quietly spoken, she always spoke well of others. I took this to be loyalty. My nan taught me to always see the best in others. That was truly admirable, however for many years, it was a cause for me to be quite vulnerable. I had a habit of taking things to extremes. Mum would say of me that I would never be half-hearted about anything. The extreme of only looking to the good in others was that I didn't see the bad in anyone. In my child-like way I had lived in a world of make believe, where everything and everyone was good. Hardly surprising that I had a few wake-up calls along life's way, especially coming to terms with my own imperfections. Nan had been the natural role model for me, and I think, for the family. Nan was the person others would come to in times of trouble.

In effect, the mental maze is the store house of those memories and emotions that have been suppressed: the situations, the experiences, the giants that we haven't been able to make sense of. They get stored away and hinder our journey through life and our mental well-being. In my case, I had been so good at doing this, that there would come a point where mentally/emotionally I couldn't take any more pain, and my mind would almost behave like the safety curtain in the theatre. The safety curtain would come down. Life in the outside world would be shut out. Medication would eventually restore balance. Life would go on. The giants remained hidden. It was a bit like Alice in Wonderland: I had been a child trying to make sense of life in an adult world.

The third giant to fall was over-respect for/fear of authority. I had grown up at home learning to respect authority, with a flawed understanding that authority was always right. I could also be intimidated by authority, which had on occasions made me very vulnerable in the workplace. A rare incident was a rather over-bearing boss. I buried my head in the sand and eventually became unwell. After all, this person was the boss, the one in authority. How did authority become a giant? The answer goes back to childhood and to Mum. I can now write this with a light heart, walking through the mental maze into freedom.

My first memory of Mum and virtually my only early childhood memory was of her flying at me, in my own words, "like someone not right." The peace and quiet of our family home had, for me, been disturbed by a knock on the front door. My brother was about three to four months old and I would be around four and a half years old at the time. There were two teenage girls at the front door, who I discovered had knocked to ask if they could take my brother out in his pram. Suddenly Mum told me to put on my hat and coat and announced that I was going out. I panicked and at that moment was afraid. All I can then remember was shouting out that I wasn't going out. I didn't need to go out. Before I could take a breath Mum flew at me, dragged me up the stairs, threw me into the bedroom and told me that I would do as I was told for the future. I broke down crying, all went black around me. I felt helpless, alone, forlorn. The next thing that happened, the bedroom door was opened, and Mum roared at me. By this time, I knew that I would have to put on my hat and coat. Staying in was not an option. My life was then cursed, as she shouted, "I'll teach you that if you disobey me, you will rue the day you were born. Just wait 'til your dad comes home. I'll tell him how naughty you've been."

A moment's anger, my life under a curse, to "rue the day I was born." I was hurriedly taken to the front door and, insult to injury, the two "strangers" began to push my brother's pram. These two strangers kindly told me that I could put a hand on the side of the pram. What kind of a message did that send to me? At the age I was, it sent a message that outsiders had a higher role than me. I had become an outcast, an outsider. This giant had stalked me all my life. True to her word, when Dad arrived home, I was reported by Mum to be the naughty daughter. For so many years, my mind would return to the moment Dad arrived home and the memory of him climbing up the stairs to the bedroom. My heart was like a lead balloon. I knew what would follow. Dad relayed to me what Mum had shared. Was I sorry for what I had done? Although I wasn't, I knew that the only way out was to tell him what he wanted to hear; that I was sorry. In my mind, authority ruled. I respected his wishes and told him I was sorry.

Years later, at a healing meeting in London, led by an American evangelist, I wept bitterly as the gathering were led in worship. "What is the matter?" asked husband Phil. "I've told a lie." I had been crippled inside at having told a lie to my dad all those years ago. A misconception around authority and a life-long fear had set in.

At that point, I had become a non-person, a person of no value, of no worth. Worthlessness was the next giant to be challenged. I very quickly learnt that I was valued by what I did and that I would be punished if I didn't do what was asked of me. How vulnerable I became. I wouldn't dream of saying "no" to anyone. It was hardly surprising as I reflect on my life's pattern that I would commit myself to just about anything and had also developed a tendency to over-work in the workplace, in that there would often be more work to do than there were hours in the day. A win-win situation for me and my employer. The workplace, in fact, became my second home. It was a place of acceptance, where I made lots of friends and was fulfilled in what I did. Equally I have retained good friendships with most of the bosses I have worked with over the years. At work, I had been valued. I had found a place of worth.

How can a giant of worthlessness be defeated? How do we stop working ourselves into the ground, repeating the same old pattern, pushing ourselves physically beyond what our bodies were designed for? What is the pathway through the maze? Quite simply believing the truth of God's word, and what His word tells us. Psalm 139:14 tells us,

> *"I praise you because I am fearfully and wonderfully made..."*

It takes some doing when we have subscribed to a lie about ourselves. Am I really "fearfully and wonderfully made"?

The way out of this giant is to persist. God's word always brings us freedom.

> *"You will know the truth and the truth will set you free"* (John 8:32).

We truly are fearfully and wonderfully made and with the help of the Holy Spirit, our Creator will set us free to be the person we were created to be. At the very least, we can sit down and ask ourselves the question, "Why do I keep punishing myself? Why am I doing this?" We possibly don't want to ask ourselves the question, because we don't want to find out the answer. It might be something even worse.

Another giant to be addressed on the journey through the maze for me was around the questions of "Who is right?" and "What is right?" "What is black, and what is white?" Again, this goes back to what we learn in our childhood. It is amazing just how much information we can store away in the early and formative years of our lives. It was many years before I was able to tackle this giant, although I did have some insight. For a time, my mind seemed a bit like "Spaghetti Junction." For anyone unfamiliar with this junction, it is a complex junction just off the M6 near Birmingham, a place where traffic can easily build up. There are many routes off this junction; the structure itself can look like a bowl of spaghetti. That's a bit like how my mind felt. I had lots of information in my head, from a variety of different sources and yet for reasons unknown at the time I had been unable to process it all.

There are keys that we are given along life's way and which come from the most unexpected sources. One such key to seeing this particular giant defeated came from a former boss as we were walking from the administration building where we were based to the main hospital building. I can't remember what the conversation was about, other than I remember my boss saying to me at some point, "Life doesn't run in straight lines, Jean." How weird was that? I had always thought that it did. Part of how we think, or how we have learnt to think over the years can in some part relate to our educational system. In my formative years, I had learnt by rote. I can see how this had possibly strengthened my ability to remember facts and remember in detail. Phil often remarks on the detail with which I can remember past events and conversations. The downside of learning by rote had been that I had never learnt in depth.

It was my time at theological college, later in life, that gave me the opportunity to think more deeply and more broadly and to be challenged by my own inbuilt, and until then, hidden, value system. This was the last and most difficult giant to navigate. Broadly speaking, I discovered that there weren't too many areas where I might have been at odds with others. However, stored away in my memory bank were those memories where "black and white" and "right and wrong" had caused both division and pain. A particularly painful memory relates to my time at commercial college. One of the subjects studied was Commerce and as part of our studies, our lecturer set up a debating session. A friend and I led opposite sides of the debate. You can imagine what happened. It transpired that at that time we had completely opposing views, which ultimately led to a falling out. Years after college, we happened to bump into one another in town. What a relief. We had both grown up and clearly those issues that had divided us had become a thing of the past.

How then was I able to deal with this giant and exit the mental maze? You might say I had to become a grown up. From my own experience, being a "grown up" over the age of eighteen, twenty-eight or even thirty-eight doesn't really have a great deal of significance. We can carry values through life, as I did for a time, without those inbuilt values necessarily being challenged. We can navigate our way through life, maybe feel a little uncomfortable at times, yet without being brave enough to take a deeper look at the different values we have taken on board, where they have come from, and how they stack up for our lives today. If we let go of those values, what will replace them? A sticking point for us can be that the values we have held so dear can also become our crutch. It can be easier to hang on to them, than to let them go. The bottom line, therefore, is compromise and we are never truly free.

How did I get free? Quite simply, by taking one step at a time. Facing one giant at a time. We don't suddenly become overwhelmed by debilitating thoughts and feelings. They build up over a series of time. And it takes time to work our way through them all. I have been blessed with a good husband, someone who loves the Lord, and one or two true friends. The last step to freedom from the mental maze was facing fear itself. What if? What if I disappointed others? What if others didn't approve of me? What if people didn't like me? What if I dug deep enough, I wouldn't even like myself? We can be afraid of what we might find if we really dig deep enough. The greatest freedom in life is to be ourselves. In my case, the person God created me to be. I can hardly believe it has taken me so long, yet it has been so worth the journey and so worth persevering.

Walking out of this mental maze, I knew for sure that I was loved by God. I knew that I had been created for a purpose. I knew that even through the dark days, the dark times, God had somehow been there, walking beside me. I could enjoy being me and in enjoying being me, I had that same freedom to enjoy/appreciate others, and encourage them, as I encourage you the reader to take that journey. The psalmist writes,

*"Thank You for making me so wonderfully complex! Your workmanship is marvellous – how well I know it"* (Psalm 139:14).

Yet, there was a further step to take.

JEAN DOBSON

## CHAPTER 8
# SELF-AWARENESS

In Chapter 7 we learnt about those events in our lives and the subsequent thoughts and feelings we can internalise. What about our outer world? What are those things that happen in life that, if we take the time to look at them, will tell us something about who we have become, the traits that we have developed and those things that we might choose to change? Having stepped out of the maze, how does the next step in life's journey take us to greater freedom?

What paths have we been tempted to take? Who have we sought to please? What are the pointers? If we search deep enough, this can lead us to the direction of travel we have taken: those who have influenced us and a realisation, underneath it all, of who we really are. We can have influences that are both good and bad. Self-realisation gives us the freedom to decide on what paths to take for the future. What advice do I need to shelve? What advice do I need to take on board? The beginnings of self-realisation. I am not bound by what pleases others.

Possibly like many people on planet earth, the early influencers in my life have been my immediate family. In my case, the two significant influencers were my nan and my dad. Again, possibly like in many families, the generation once removed was of significant interest – the older generation have been it, done it, and were a source of experience and wisdom. For me, my nan was no exception. Always calm, always at peace. As you will have gathered, my nan was someone I loved dearly and was a great source of knowledge and, for me, inspiration. Possibly like many granddaughters before me, I was keen to know more about her earlier years. What shape did life take in those days? From what Nan shared with me I had a picture of ideal family life. Everyone had a role to play within the family, each one differently gifted, each one adding something to the family. The family lived in what was known as "The Old Vicarage" in Melling. It was just down the road from the family place of worship, St Thomas and the Holy Rood (a story in itself). I had pictures in my mind of the family walking to church in their long dresses and over the fields to the nearest railway station to take the train into Liverpool.

Such was the impression I had, that I had to go out to Melling to see the family home for myself. I have a collection of photographs taken of the family and the outside of the family home. I had to explore. Just before Phil and I married, I took him out to Melling to show him the place of my dreams. I stepped along the path to the front door and peeped in through one of the windows. Suddenly a lady came to the front door – the owner. I no sooner apologised for trespassing than we were invited in. The lady explained that since she and her husband had bought the property, they had had many visitors like me, all of whom had links with the building. A special surprise, the week before Phil and I married I visited St Thomas for the morning family communion service. To my surprise, I was introduced to a lady who had known my nan and the family, mentioning different ones by name. It was the icing on the cake. It was a link to the family I had learnt so much about.

Years down the line, Mum shared a different side of the story. As the family had grown, so had challenges and different views that for Mum had brought both division and heartache. It was devastating news for me and for a time I lived with the heartache of a burst bubble. I realised over time, that for Nan it didn't. Nan never saw the differences, rather the possibilities that broken relationships could be healed. There was always the possibility of reconciliation. Different people can have different views, different perspectives on life. I understood where Mum's perspective had come from. For years I was unable to reconcile both accounts. What Nan had shared was what was in her heart. What was in her heart was what she had drawn from her Christian faith. That couldn't be taken away.

Family life was so very different from Mum's perspective, with the added challenges of a second world war. Lives had been lost to war and families torn apart. What I became aware of was that as far as Mum was concerned, life had been far from ideal. There had been challenges within family life, disagreements and almost a falling-out between different members of the family. On the surface, all appeared to be within reason. I found myself in the middle of two different opinions, Mum for sure pressing for her side "to be right." It caused me a great deal of heartache and weighed heavily on my mind, particularly after Nan's earthly journey had come to an end. I had wanted everyone to be happy. The harsh realisation was that apparently not everyone was happy. What I had learnt from my nan stayed with me. We all make mistakes, life can go a bit pear-shaped, yet we can learn to live together, accepting our differences. What did I learn for myself through that process? Quite simply, that I will never be everyone's friend. In the worst possible scenario, I might be no-one's friend. The importance here is one of integrity, that I learnt to be true to myself. I was aware of what was important to me, even if it was costly.

The second and biggest single influencer was my dad. Like my nan, for most part my dad was a calming influence on family life. Dad's philosophy on life was that "it will all work out right in the end." I realised over time that this was from a simple faith, a simple outlook on life that my dad had held close to his heart. Unlike Mum, who was brought up in a strong and confident family, Dad's family experience was significantly different. Dad's grandmother had died in childbirth. Dad's grandfather had died of a broken heart within twelve months. The upshot was that Dad's mum was brought up by her aunt, her mum's sister. Whilst raised within that family, Dad's mum was always made aware that she had been adopted into the family – an outsider brought in. Dad's parents met when his mum had been the housekeeper in his dad's home. It was shock horror when grandad married grandma. He was disowned by the family. A sadness passed on down to my dad.

What impact did that have on me? Quite simply that family life for Dad had been quite different to that of Mum and yet family remained as important to me then as it does now. Family life has its challenges and no more so than when two people from two different families marry. How did they meet in the first place? At school. Mum, Dad, her brother and cousin all attended the local infant/junior school. They were from local families. How could two people like Mum and Dad, who had come from two very different backgrounds, establish a home life into which both I and my brother had been born? The answer is that it was not without its challenges. Mum's side of the family had all been small businesspeople, successful in what they did. They had a confidence, not an arrogance, and I always enjoyed their company. I found them to be interesting in their different ways, and as a group, they were the biggest single influence on my life.

On the other side of the coin, family life had been so very different; Dad had been born into relative poverty. Such was the difference between both families, that on Mum's side, the family had a genuine concern that Dad would not be able to provide for Mum. On the face of it, that seemed reasonable. Their concern was such that some members of the family tried to persuade her not to marry him, offering her a considerable sum of money to stay single. Can you imagine the impact that would have had on her? As I have been able to reflect, I have been able to appreciate some of the challenge my parents faced on their wedding day, especially for Mum. On a July day it rained. The turnout for the wedding was amazing. Mum's side of the family were well-known and respected locally. Imagine what it would be like to walk down the aisle, with the knowledge that some members of the family were not sure that you were doing the right thing. I have a gut feeling that some of those dark thoughts that had hung over me, had hung over her on her wedding day. Wouldn't we all hope that the person we choose to marry would be accepted by the wider family?

For myself, I had to face challenges around marriage

twice over. For my first marriage to Norman and with my Church of England background, there was the question as to whether someone who had not previously been married should marry a divorced person. The second question for me was how I, as a widow, would be received by the family of the eldest son I was to marry? Philip was, without doubt to me, something of the shining star to his widowed mother. Both Phil and his brother Andrew were active in church life, with Phil taking a leadership role. I was never quite sure how his mum would take to "Number One" son marrying a widow. Note to self: each one of us has a life to live, whether what we do, what we say, and how we respond to situations is well received by others, integrity to ourselves is so important. Phil and I were quite sure that to marry was the right thing for both of us. The last thirty-four years have told their own story. We prayed a lot, we wanted to be sure we were doing the right thing. Marriage is such a big step in life. As I reflect on the last thirty-four years, I have no doubt that we both made the right decision.

For someone who had some very odd thoughts about married life, to have been married, widowed and to re-marry was quite remarkable. Having shared the challenge Mum faced in marrying Dad, the different life experience of the two families, the different aspirations, I realised that all this had had quite an impact on my thinking. Marriage brought controversy. Marriage brought conditions. Marriage was disruptive. Who would want all that hassle? Who would want to get dressed up for the day anyway? It took quite some journey, and a work of grace for me to realise that this was something that God had instituted with very good purpose.

Back to Dad and his influence on my life. When I look at my parent's wedding photographs I see such a vulnerable young man. He was dressed in his Air Force uniform, just twenty-one years old, preparing to head out for war. I've always been drawn to his jacket which had long sleeves, touching down to his fingers. The image didn't do him justice. Despite early family reservations, he fitted in well and was liked by the whole family. Dad was never going to head up a major bank, however he worked hard and as a family we survived.

Dad always encouraged me as best he could. By nature, he was quite passive: a home bird who just wanted a quiet life. Dad would go out of his way not to cause offence to anyone. Whilst Mum was, by nature, a pro-active person, Dad was very passive and someone who just wanted to get through life. Hidden behind a calm exterior, I sensed a sadness, almost a disappointment, hidden on the inside. It was hidden, as always by a brave face. Sometimes, without realising it, we pick things up. We sense a sadness, a disappointment, without words being spoken. From what I learnt from Mum, that wasn't without reason. Dad had faced many disappointments. Our early beginnings can impact how we set out on life's journey, with the expectation of succeeding or failing. I sensed that for Dad it was the latter. This was such a contrast to Mum's life experience, yet it taught me to have compassion. Dad was loved and accepted by Mum's family, despite their concerns at the outset. The concerns were never about Dad as a person, rather his ability to "earn a good wage." "Would he be able to provide for her?" He was never going to be a macho-man. Dad was a plodder who got through life, who I loved just the same. A gentle, to me, uncomplicated man, who nevertheless made his mark on life. It did, however, have a negative impact on me, which we will come back to.

Probably the hardest lesson I have had to learn is facing my own weaknesses and my inability to meet the expectations of others. We set off in life with a set of guidelines around us, rules to live by and without realising it, we set ourselves up to fail. I distinctly remember a conversation with Dad, one Sunday morning, returning home from church. I can't remember the exact conversation, other than we got round to the question of the ten commandments. I remember Dad saying to me, "As long as you keep the ten commandments, you will be alright." My heart sank – I had failed!

One of my biggest weaknesses was that I couldn't bear to see pain in others. It took me a long time to realise that I couldn't make people better, nor relieve their pain. I think because of something of the pain and heartache I had seen in my own family, I would be drawn to the pain in others. Within church life there can be so many hurting people. During these times, Phil showed remarkable patience. You have no idea of the number of visits I would make, the number of phone calls I would take, listening to people for hours at a time. As with work, I would run myself into the ground, trying to help others. Despite being a Christian and understanding the teaching of scripture, it has taken me a long time to realise that I have worth and that I have to care for myself. My life has equal importance. This could well go back to the early childhood memory of feeling worthless. Without realising it, we can run ourselves into the ground, trying to turn around a thought that has crept into our minds. At a level most people try to help others. For me, there had been a hidden and quite unconscious need to desperately do enough to give myself a feeling of worth. One day I might be a person of worth.

A second weakness I learnt about myself came via an extraordinary route. For a number of years, I had been based at the rear of the building where I worked. There was a long corridor from the back to the front of the building. I would regularly have to make trips to the reception area in the front of the building. The girls would tell me they always knew when I was approaching reception, as they could hear my footsteps approaching at high speed. I thought it was hilarious. I was always going at high speed. The word "slow" hadn't featured in my vocabulary. One day I thought about this. Why was I always running? What was I running away from? The answer? Me! Underneath, I had been living with my failures. Equally, I realised that I had been guilty of something quite unexpected. Being close to my nan, without me realising, I had allowed my nan to become something of an idol and the perfect human being. I had wanted to be like her. As best I knew, she had never done anything wrong and never spoke a bad word about anyone. Realisation set in: It would never happen in a million years that I would ever be like my nan. In temperament alone, we were very different. We were born at different times into different cultures, different education and into a very different world. Nan had had to navigate its challenges. I had my own to navigate. I would never succeed trying to be a replica of her, or anyone else for that matter.

The next weakness was intimidation. I had been very easily intimidated by people with strong personalities and loud voices, particularly women. I would run a mile rather than be in their company. A loud voice would set alarm bells ringing. I would jump at the sound. A bit like my dad, I would avoid conflict. Avoiding conflict resulted in compromise. I had been trapped by compromise for so long. I resented both these weaknesses. That was until they pointed me to something else. Both these weaknesses pointed me back to childhood and to an underlying emotion of fear. A way forward was to be brave enough to ask myself the question: "Why was I intimidated, why should I fear?".

A step to freedom along the way was a lady by the name of Jackie Bowler. This is another long story – not for now. Jackie was an accredited Assemblies of God minister and at the time we met was the Regional Director of Women's ministries. By default, I became the Regional Secretary. Jackie was a confident and bold woman. Did I need to be afraid? Jackie had such a heart for women, to encourage women that they could become all they were meant to be. An accomplished musician, church leader and a grandmother, Jackie was someone to behold. Her mantra: "You're a winning woman." I heard that so many times, that I eventually won through. It really was a challenge. A particular occasion comes to mind: Jackie had invited me to a women's conference in Manchester. Around one thousand women were present. My first thought was "Help! Dear Lord, get me out of here!" He didn't. Early memories don't necessarily define our lives. There are opportunities that come our way that can lead us on the path to freedom. Just one moment in time, one childhood memory, and a fear of women, authority, and what authority might do to harm me, had taken root. It was some time before I realised that that was unrealistic and that I would only be hurt and intimidated if I gave room to those thoughts. With sufficient meaningful encounters with women through the years, that misconception was put to flight.

These were the significant weaknesses in my life. There may be others I haven't identified in this book. Put simply: facing our weaknesses is not a weakness, but a strength. What I've realised, as I've written, is what the culture was like in which I grew up and the effect that it had not only on me, but also on my parents and grandparents. My early childhood had been lived out in "Great Britain" where Britain had been an expanding empire. As best I understand, much emphasis was placed on our successes. I had an inbuilt, and yet hidden, understanding that strength and success were both important. We were a strong and "successful" nation. There was no place for weakness. Weakness is a part of human frailty. Facing our weaknesses is strength in itself and a significant step into freedom.

JEAN DOBSON

## CHAPTER 9
# THE JIGSAW PIECES
**Freedom is just around the corner**

Time to come up for air – freedom is just around the corner. When the unexpected in life happens, life itself can seem to fall apart. The fact that we are living and breathing tells us that all is not lost. Life may not be the quality it once was, however, that can all change. We have clues and memories, like random jigsaw pieces that need to be put together. There was one big hurdle I had to get over before I was able to start putting the pieces together.

That seemingly insurmountable hurdle was the one painful memory, the one moment when, for me, it all began to go pear-shaped. As already shared, the earliest memory of Mum was my life being cursed. How could I possibly challenge authority? The "Ten Commandments" also presented a significant challenge for me. The fifth in order of these commandments reads,

*"Honour your father and your mother"* (Exodus 20:12).

As a child, I had mistakenly understood honour to mean authority that was never to be questioned. It took me a long time to understand that honour meant something quite different: more to show respect. I have always loved and respected my parents.

My mistake was to take on board the misconception that

because they were my parents, everything they said and did was "right." Childlike understanding. It was hardly surprising that there was a point where I ended up at a place called "Confused.com" – the Spaghetti Junction I have previously referenced. Alongside this was another weakness I had taken on board. Basically, I would excuse everything by reasoning and logical thinking. In effect, what I was doing was being passive – a trait I may well have picked up from my dad. "It will all work out alright in the end," he would say. How had I reasoned out that incident? I had been naughty, Mum had lost her temper, life happens, move on. The reality was life had moved on, but I hadn't. Somehow, there was a blockage. My life was moving forward, yet not flowing as best it should. I knew there was a frustration underneath. I just hadn't been able to identify what it was. Every time I looked at photographs of my childhood, I could see there was something hidden: two and two just weren't making four.

How could that hurdle be overcome? The first step forward was realising a pattern, that whenever my thoughts spiralled down to that one memory, I would hit pain. It was almost unbearable. If only it hadn't happened. It had and the pain hadn't gone away. I knew there was something wrong; something that I couldn't fix myself. As part of my development at work, I had been put on a counselling course. On one occasion course members were asked to share a particular painful memory/difficult situation. When it came to my turn, I shard the childhood memory that had haunted me. The suggestion came "Couldn't you just re-write it?" How could I? How could I pretend something hadn't happened and write myself a happy ending? I couldn't. The good news is that someone could – the happy ending was just around the corner.

Significant to my story are three other factors. The first was the Christmas card I referred to earlier. The beaming Father Christmas with two toys seated on his lap. A picture of Father God, who loved His creation. The toys spoke to me of a previous era, Edwardian England. Overall, at the centre was a God who loved us, however the toys spoke to me of authority, and presented a challenge. I couldn't seem to get away from authority. I had taken one small step forward.

The second step held more significance. One night I had a dream. I pictured myself in southern Spain (a place close to my heart). It was early in the evening, and I was peering through some beautiful ornate metal gates. At the far end I could see a party taking place. It reminded me of a setting something like "The Last Supper" which Jesus ate with His disciples. I was being invited to join in. I kept peering through the gates. The evening was warm, the gathering was both joyful and inviting. I wanted to accept the invitation, yet I was hesitant. I woke up – still peering through the gates, longing to accept the invitation and join in.

The third factor, yet the most unexpected, was a key to freedom and a follow-on from my dream. I have used the word "unexpected" several times throughout this book, and with purpose. It was the unexpected that had thrown me, that had seemingly almost thrown my life off course. It was the "unexpected" moments, the moments when I sensed God's presence that would bring correction, understanding and would firmly set the dial for my life due North. This third factor relates to a Christian gathering in Frodsham. The gathering takes place monthly and is known as "The Big Push." It's a ministry led by a dear friend, Sue Sinclair. From the picture I had had of myself peering through gates and resisting an invitation to join in, the invitation came again, in a different way at this meeting. At one point, a member of The Big Push team stepped forward and shared that the Lord was inviting us to "come to Him." He was calling us forward. It was time to pay attention. He was calling me forward to accept an invitation. I sat in my seat. I knew I had to respond. What was holding me back? As an intercessor, I was regularly in His presence for others. I absolutely loved praying for others. What on earth was holding me back?

Suddenly, revelation came. I saw myself locked in a prison, a prison from which I couldn't escape. Strangely, the word prison held a specific meaning for me. It wasn't what you might think! In the book of Acts (Acts 16:31) there is the account of a man known as the Philippian jailer. It became, for me, a promise from scripture that as I believed in God for my salvation, so too my family would also be saved. I had an absolute assurance. True to His word, I had seen each of my three family members come through to salvation before they died. Back to prison. No sooner had that picture come to mind than the penny dropped. I had been imprisoned by Mum's words. Equally I had expected an explanation, at the very least from Mum that there would be a recognition that possibly she had acted in haste. And a word from Sue: "Do we need to forgive someone who wasn't sorry for that they had done and the apology I never received?" Two and two made four and the penny dropped. The significance of life not running in straight lines hit home.

As soon as I realised the apology was never going to

come, the prison door opened and I was free. Words are powerful and they carry life or death. The power of God is even greater. In that moment, I was set free. And so the happy ending came that had evaded me for so long. The power of those words had been broken and I truly was free. The painful memory had gone, in an instant. Yes, my life had been cursed and Mum never remembered the words she had spoken. An apology was never going to come. I had been taught, if you have made a mistake, you need to say sorry. That was, unless you were an adult. Authority could never be questioned.

That was my biggest hurdle. From that moment on, everything began to fit into place. One by one I was able to pick up the pieces of the jigsaw puzzle that had been my life. Even greater had been the ability to write this book, several years after Mum has made her journey heavenward. There is a poem that some of you will be aware of, "The Divine Weaver" in which the author (unknown) references God as the Divine Weaver, weaving out the tapestry of life. In essence, good and bad things happen in life. Overall God is working out His purposes which brings me to a significant point in my journey to freedom.

The jigsaw speaks to me of God's perfect plan for our lives. It's a perfect plan which is so much bigger than anything that can come our way to try to disrupt. I can write this, after all I have been through, to assure you, the reader, that the same God who is at work in my life, will also work good out of your life. There is no situation, no problem too big or too small that He can't solve. It may not be in the way we would hope, however He will do a far better job than ever you or I could. He will get it right.

You will have gathered from what I have written that the biggest single factor at work in my life is my faith, a gift, for which I can take no credit.

The mention of faith has caused me to pick up another piece of the puzzle. Another "unexpected" moment. One Sunday evening, I was on my way to our church's monthly praise night. It was during the winter months. It was dark and on the route I had taken there were uneven paving stones. I was rushing and tripped. I arrived at church with a bleeding and swollen top lip, which continued to swell as the night went on. It just happened that I had an appointment for an annual check-up at my doctors' practice that week. I turned up for my check-up. For the first time ever, from memory, my blood pressure was sufficiently high that the practice nurse asked me to stay behind to be seen by one of the doctors in the practice.

Yes, my blood pressure was up. The weirdest conversation ensued with a doctor I had never met before. "You do realise," he said, "that we will now need to register the fact that you have presented with high blood pressure. This may affect future holidays." Without a moment's thought, my response was: "That won't bother me." However, I came away with the question "What would?" My GP gave me the option to monitor my blood pressure over three weeks, which I found fascinating. I presented the results, as requested, and a phone call from my GP confirmed that my blood pressure was "back to normal." How was my own question answered? What had bothered me? Over the three weeks I recorded my blood pressure readings and the answer came. It was a conflict around faith. In the one home, I had been faced with two different opinions. I realised that the issue was not for me to resolve. Whatever the issue for anyone else, faith was my journey to pursue.

As I pick up yet another jigsaw piece, I can also share a memory of great joy. The joy came in taking Mum on a holiday abroad for her eightieth birthday. My brother didn't think she would go. Colin really was surprised when we called him from southern Spain and put Mum on the phone. As I have previously mentioned seeing myself a little like Alice in Wonderland, trying to make sense of the adult world, the moment when she spoke to my brother from Spain, it was almost like the situation in reverse. Mum was just like the child in my adult world, so enjoying her Spanish holiday. The expression etched on her face as she spoke to my brother said something like "Guess where I am, guess what I am doing?" Such childlike joy.

The holiday went down so well, that we took her again the following year. I can hardly describe the joy. There was a German family living in the apartment next door to the one we had rented. They took Mum to heart. What fun she had as we toddled off to the local pool for a swim! How amazing, even at that time, with that painful memory locked away, that I had the best time ever seeing her enjoy an experience of life she had previously never had. It was the icing on the cake that holiday. We would hire videos to watch a film in the evening. I can't remember what the video was on this occasion, other than at one moment, to my utter surprise, Mum jumped up off her seat and began dancing round the room with me, singing "Waltzing, waltzing, waltzing with you." It was a precious moment in my life. So out of character. Mum who was always busy, always working, always keeping everything in order and this disciplined lady was suddenly dancing freely around the room with me. I can assure you, for that to have happened, shows that God can do anything.

It was another significant jigsaw piece and testimony to there being nothing too difficult for God. There is no situation He won't turn around and make good out of. There is no painful memory that He can't heal. I have shared how I wept uncontrollably at Mum's funeral and that Phil kindly put everything in place for me. Through all the tears, as I pick up that particular piece of the jigsaw, I marvel at the joyful pictures we were able to show of her life, particularly the holidays Phil, Mum and I had been on. We had never had a holiday as a family. It had never bothered me. That's how life was. What a difference prayer had made, what joy she had had in those latter years. Without question of doubt, Spain held the happiest of memories. I had never known her to be so happy and so free. I can honestly say that I know my heavenly Father knows me inside out, as I look back on those happy days. It had all happened without me even realising.

So significant are those last two years. I had grown up never having had that kind of relationship with her. Nor had she with her mum. Authority was to be respected. My memories, prior to those last two years, were all ones of being sent out by her – out to play, out to visit family members, mostly Nan's sisters. I was always sent out somewhere. I didn't mind – I mostly enjoyed all the places I went to and the people I spent time with. One challenge wasn't being allowed to help in the home. My friends had household chores, like cleaning/tidying their bedrooms each week. I wasn't allowed to do anything. When asking could I help, I was told, "Time enough for you to do housework when you have to." It set a mystique around housework. I became quite ignorant when it came to domestic life. There were times, as I and my friends grew up, that I would feel the "odd one out." I was the last one to marry. My friends would talk about the latest cooker, best washing powder, etc. I was completely out of it. Without a doubt I felt odd, uncomfortable at my ignorance. There was something wrong with me. Does that ring a bell? Yes, they were the only words I could speak to my nan when she came to visit me in hospital. "Nan, there's something wrong with me."

The bottom line is, there's something wrong with all of us. We all start life as flawed human beings. The good news is that there is Someone who can turn that around, who can take hold of the "something" that is wrong and put it right. God has a perfect plan for our lives. The flaws, the mistakes, the misunderstandings, are all things which God can take hold of and work for His good. If we can take hold of the fact that there is a perfect plan for us, then we can begin to assemble the jigsaw pieces. Dashed hopes and dashed dreams can be part of the crazy paving, the road to freedom, to be the person we were meant to be. We simply need to be ready to start the journey.

Neither you nor I were designed to be like someone else. We are all unique, and part of the journey to freedom is finding the uniqueness in which we have been created and the purpose God has for our lives. Like with a jigsaw puzzle, we start with the picture on the front of the box. Bit by bit we put the pieces together. Some pieces fit together more easily, some can take much longer, some need to be put to one side. Bit by bit, momentum grows, and eventually the whole jigsaw comes together.

JEAN DOBSON

## CHAPTER 10
# FREEDOM

What does freedom look like? How do we get there? Is the journey worth the effort? Freedom for me looks like I've won the pools a thousand times over, every day of my life. How did I get there? I have given a brief outline in this book. It wasn't an easy journey, yet there was something inside me that told me the journey had to be pursued. Was it worth the effort? Yes, yes and yes again.

As I write this final chapter, I am reminded of a young child who came to what was known as our "Parents and Tots" group. It was an activity that we ran for the young mums within our church community. This young child was the great nephew of the elder who led the group. He, and one of the friends he made, loved to be chased. I thoroughly enjoyed chasing them and giving them a run for their money. Fond memories were recalled of the time when two of my nan's sisters used to chase me! One afternoon, I was told this young child said to his mum, "I'm going to get that big girl in the kitchen." What a compliment that was. In his mind I was the big girl in the kitchen. After helping to serve refreshments and washing up, I was free to help interact with the children, giving the mums a rest and an opportunity to chat together. Playing with the children brought me great joy.

This young child's enthusiasm so reminded me of myself and my determination to "get God." My nan had told me all about Him. My journey had been to find Him for myself. On reflection, it had at times been something of a perilous journey. There had been obstacles in the way. Nothing unusual here. The early church faced significantly greater challenges than I had.

An important part of the journey was the issue of medication. There is no shame in taking medication, although there were times when I wanted to be the super-hero and demonstrate that I didn't need medication. My mind, after all, wasn't controlled by chemicals. I couldn't wait to discontinue medication – to swim without armbands. The problem was that not long after the armbands had been removed, I would discover that I couldn't swim. I learnt an odd lesson about our body chemistry and how it worked, as ever in an unexpected way. A very close friend was in hospital, terminally ill. I had had a phone call from my friend's daughter to let me know that her mum was in hospital with a brain tumour, which had grown and was impairing speech. I was encouraged to be prepared for a visit. Roberta and I might not be able to have a conversation.

As ever, I prayed, then headed off to hospital. Both Roberta's two grown-up children were at her bedside. I arrived, and our conversation took up, as it always did, from the last time we had met. It was such a good visit. Afterwards, my friend's daughter explained that there had been a change in Roberta's medication from the phone call I had received to my visit. Roberta had been prescribed a maximum dose of steroids which had reduced the swelling around the brain, hence releasing freedom to speak. It really was food for thought. As best I understand, there are some sixty chemicals in the human body and what all of them are doing is yet to be discovered. The brain, the mind, how did they interact? Again, as best I understand, the brain is a physical organ in our head which supports the functions of our mind to think, feel and to engage in physical activity.

I have often thought that as tripartite human beings, what happens in one part has an impact on the other two. By tripartite I mean we comprise three parts – spirit, soul and body. As a child, my spirit had been broken, my soul wounded and the wounds kept coming. The upshot of all that I had internalised and had not even allowed myself to think about, was without doubt, a recipe for a chemical meltdown and a nervous breakdown. All that had been repressed internally had to find expression, one way or another. As a Christian, why had I never spoken to God about it all? Quite simply, at that point in my life I didn't have the understanding that I have now. A mark of freedom is to eventually be able to do so. Our Father always has time for us, is always willing to listen. The death of His Son would be nonsense if that were not the case.

With what I realise now, I had developed a subservient attitude to life. I had without appreciating it taken to heart my responsibilities in church life. I would do anything and everything that was required of me. I wondered where it would all take me. Nowhere was the answer. Another mark of freedom is being able to make that necessary change. It's important to recognise a behavioural pattern that isn't necessarily helpful and have the courage to make that change. I remember a time in hospital when another patient would sing to me a well-known country and western song "One day at a time." Years later, those same words came back to me and as I write, they are on a poster on our conservatory wall.

I was reminded not all that long ago by a dear friend from church, "Jean, you are doing far too much. Take life one day at a time." Hence the poster on our conservatory wall. The point here is that we need to make a determined effort to maintain the freedom we find for ourselves. There can always appear to be a reason why we should do 101 things, and we can be tempted to go back to an old restrictive way of life. Breathe in freedom and enjoy the moment. Be determined not to go back. It may take one or two attempts. I am sure, like me, you will have at least one friend along the way who will be just the prompt you need.

Does freedom mean I can do whatever I like? Of course not. Quite the opposite, it gives us the freedom not to do what others might expect of us, or what we think they might expect of us. We can have an inbuilt desire to overcompensate for the mistakes we have made, to not have been the son or daughter we think our parents might have wanted us to be. I had to follow Jesus. I couldn't do what Mum wanted me to do. It may sound ridiculous. I know she wanted only the best for me and both my parents did their very best for me to have the best life I could. Mum's biggest fear was that I would end up with "religious mania." Another story for another time. I am no hero. I would have liked to have been a better daughter, whatever that would mean. The result of the choice I made was that she too, eventually became free. Mum could see that my prayer life wasn't making me ill, nor was being part of church life. Rather the opposite. Mum's fear of prayer, or more of God and what He might do, disappeared as over time she saw my faith grow and would ask me to pray for her friends and neighbours.

Freedom sets us free from fear. Fear is often described as "False Evidence Appearing Real." Fear can be described as an emotion caused by a potential threat of danger, pain or harm. How do we become free of fear? What emotion is said to be stronger than fear? Surprise, surprise: love itself. Fear can appear to be so much stronger than love, depending on how we have experienced either. For instance, I would get birthday and Christmas cards from Mum and Dad, always signed, "Love, Mum and Dad." I had no idea what that meant. There had been no tangible expression of love from either throughout my childhood. I had never actually been told that I was loved. What I knew most was if I obeyed the rules, I would stay out of trouble. Most likely it was the same for my parents. There was no outward expression of love for them. They just simply followed the rules. Fear however had become very real – I knew the consequences if I didn't follow the rules. It was simply a pattern of life that had been passed down through generations.

How can love itself be greater? Quite simply, by being experienced. In my case, it has been experiencing God's love for me, which is unconditional. I know that I am loved unconditionally, which by its very nature is reciprocal. How could I not love someone who loves me so much that His son would die on a cross to pay the price of my sin, my mistakes that at one time would separate me from God. I had not known any different.

Without question of doubt, the one person who has made that understanding possible for me was dear Freddie,

Father Freddie to his congregation. From that very first conversation we had, when Freddie described God's love to me, what it looked like, a journey began in my understanding of what love really was like. It was pure, it was perfect and it could be experienced. There were many occasions, over the years, when I had occasion to be in London and there was the opportunity to meet Freddie over a coffee. I knew for sure that Freddie knew God, that God truly was a kind and loving God. The Bible tells us that

*"God is love"* (1 John 4:8).

That same passage of scripture addresses fear. In 1 John 4:18 it says,

*"There is no fear in love; but perfect love casts out all fear."*

Fear has to do with punishment and seeks to take root in our mind.

Without me realising, fear had taken root in my mind, and had had a crippling effect on my life over many years. Fear has gone, the love of God has taken its place with the understanding of who God really is. The book of the New Testament is full of the miracles that Jesus performed, the sick who were healed, the lame who walked, the dead brought back to life. Could a troubled mind, a mind that had been clouded by debilitating thoughts and feelings be too big a challenge for our God? Absolutely not. With a thankful heart, I can truly say "freedom at last."

The same could be true for you.

# CONCLUSION

Well done as you reach this final page and thank you for journeying with me. My hope is that the conversation on mental health will open more widely. One of my hesitations in putting pen to paper was simply that I could only write as a Christian. Would anyone be interested? Is being a Christian and having to battle through deeply troubling thoughts and feelings synonymous with faith? What I have realised as I have written is that we in the western world can be a little sceptical of anything "spiritual." I am not a religious person – far from it. My faith is a spiritual experience. Like everyone else I am a flawed human being who has recognised my need of a Saviour. I am a flawed and broken human being, put back together again by a living and loving God.

In a world where there appears to be a quick fix for everything and a product to buy that allegedly meets a need of self-worth, why search further? The bottom line is none of these truly meet a deeper need within. In our search for significance, where do we go? I have mentioned the jigsaw puzzle which probably most of us have come across at some stage. We look at the front of the box, see the picture, then empty out the contents and set about creating the image we have seen on the box. When I was younger, I needed a little help. I would get so far, then call on my dad. For us as human beings as we navigate our way through life, we need a picture, an idea, a framework to work to. How do I fit into the bigger picture? What is the picture you had of your life when you started out?

I believe that God has created the world we live in, and that from what I have seen, He has done a great job. In a perfect world, how do I fit in? I would at one time pride myself on being a perfectionist – I was going to do the perfect job. I always had to be perfect. None of us are perfect. Coming to terms with our flaws and imperfections can be the hardest thing ever, yet in that place of realisation, we can find true freedom. I was never made to be perfect. I was made in the image of God,

> *"So God created human beings in His own image"* (Genesis 1:27).

*He has a plan and a purpose for my life.*

> *"For I know the plans I have for you, says the Lord. They are plans for good and not for disaster, to give you a future and a hope"* (Jeremiah 29:11).

It has taken me a long time to get here; to recognise that I am made in the likeness and image of God and made for His purpose. For me it became a place of true freedom. The Creator of the whole world has a purpose and a plan for my life. As my dad helped me put together the jigsaw pieces, so the person of the Holy Spirit has helped me navigate life, to see the bigger picture and the purpose for my life as I daily read His word.

My prayer for you is that you too will find the freedom I have found. I pray you will have mental health, freedom from those dark thoughts and from those feelings that are only obstacles to be overcome. There is a life to be enjoyed.

# ABOUT THE AUTHOR

Jean Dobson started her life from humble beginnings. Born post-war in Liverpool, the biggest spiritual influence was her maternal grandmother who told her about a good God who created the world that we live in. This was the beginnings of a journey of faith. From her time at a local commercial college, Jean's basic administrative gift was honed, which opened many and varied doors in the workplace. On marriage to Phil, ministry doors opened, which included co-leading an Assemblies of God church in inner city Toxteth, ministering to the small church congregation and the wider community of the homeless men and women living in hostels nearby. Jean has a passion for prayer and to see the broken healed through God's amazing love.

JEAN DOBSON

Printed in Poland
by Amazon Fulfillment
Poland Sp. z o.o., Wrocław